Praise for
More Than Words Can Say: The Making of Inspired Speakers

This small but powerful book towers well above the typical "Make yourself a better Public Speaker" offering. It is a blend of philosophy, psychology, and communication that, in a word, works. Saskia advises us to tell a story with simplicity and sincerity.

Clearly, she knows how to follow her own advice.

Public Speaking, as she might tell you, is not an activity like hitting a golf ball or following a culinary recipe. It is more than having expertise and facility. It must begin with "knowing yourself," before asking others to receive your message and understand who you are.

I only wish this book had been around many years ago at the outset of my teaching and consulting career. But "better late than never..."

Leonard G. Schifrin
Chancellor Professor of Economics, Emeritus
College of William and Mary

~ ~ ~

More Than Words Can Say *reminds that silence and listening are the building blocks for effective public speaking. This book challenges us to apply these simple principles, then effortlessly convinces that public speaking can and should be a joy. Every lawyer who is preparing a jury trial, or even a short, educational or persuasive piece, should read* More Than Words Can Say.

Craig M. Notte, Esq.
Borah, Goldstein, Altschuler, Nahins & Goidel, P.C.
New York, New York

~ ~ ~

Saskia has written a book that every actor should carry around 24/7. It is a concise and precise reminder of the foundation for acting, often overlooked as we pursue our art and our careers. Her words, "Forget about performing, and think about Being," should be the mantra for each and every actor.

Stass Klassen
Actor, Managing Artistic Director
New York Art Theatre

~ ~ ~

In running a conference company, I often say to my staff, "Pretend you are throwing a dinner party; the food and décor are important, but it's the conversation that matters most." More Than Words Can Say *shows us that while content may be king… connection to your audience is paramount!*

I wish every one of the than more 20,000 speakers who have spoken at a CBI conferences would have had the opportunity to read More than Words Can Say…*they would have benefited profoundly, both personally and professionally.*

Kathy Coffey
President
The Center for Business Intelligence

More Than Words Can Say...

The Making of Inspired Speakers

SASKIA SHAKIN

Ovation Publishers

New York, New York

First printing 2008

ISBN 978-0-9816970-3-1

LCCN 2008928506

ATTENTION CORPORATIONS, UNIVERSITIES, COLLEGES, AND PROFESSIONAL ORGANIZA-TIONS: Quantity discounts are available on bulk purchases of this book for educational, gift purposes, or as premiums for increasing magazine subscriptions or renewals. Special books or book excerpts can also be created to fit specific needs. For information, please contact Ovation Publishers, 152 West 77th St., #8., New York, NY 10024; (212) 724-7547.

For Tolya...

Who embodied the life of the theatre,

Who truly grasped the theatre of life,

And who enriched my life

More than words can say...

Table of Contents

Acknowledgments vii

I. THE BUILDING BLOCKS

Introduction 3
Who Should Read This? 5
What Is This Book About? 7
The Secret to Public Speaking 11
"The Silent Way" 13
The Second Secret to Public Speaking 17
The Law of Attraction: What You See Is What You Get 19
Vision + Values = Voice 23
Confidence: What It Is; What It Isn't 29
Do You Have Three Legs? What All Speakers Must Share .. 31
The Clever vs. the Wise 37
On a Personal Note 39
The Quiet Side of Speaking 45

II. THE BASICS

Our Two Brains 51
There's Nobody Out There But You! 53
Private Dialogue vs. Public Monologue 55
When Does a Chat Turn Into a Speech? 57
Performance Anxiety 59
What If. 63
What Next. 65
Growing Old/Growing Up 67
The Devil Is in the Details 71
The 7 Percent Solution: Substance vs. Style 75

Writer's Block: Two Kinds 79

Getting Real: The Key to Communicating 83

Serious Fun 85

III. THE DETAILS

Tell Me a Story: If You Don't, I Won't Listen! 89

The Theme vs. the Point 93

The Perfect Analogy 95

The Ear vs. the Eye 99

Eye Contact: It's Not a Spectator Sport 103

Our Spirit vs. Our Brain 105

Too Busy for Words 111

Hidden Dimensions 115

Famous Last Words 117

Yoga and Public Speaking 119

Future Goals vs. Present Action 123

In the Beginning. 125

PowerPoint vs. Personal Power 133

Can Numbers Tell Stories? 137

IV. IT'S A WRAP

A Note on the Keynote 143

Hecklers and Other Blessings 147

The Lesson in a Nightmare 149

Henry and Oprah 151

Saskia's Secrets 153

"And in Conclusion. . ." 155

Bibliography 157

Index 161

Acknowledgments

It is often said that it takes a village to raise a child...or to write a book. In my case, it has not taken a village but, rather, a lifetime.

Writing was the easy part: knowing *what* to write and *how* was where the work lay.

So it is with gratitude and love that I thank my early readers—not only for their cheerleading but for not closing down their phone lines when I called for the fourteenth time asking, "What do you think of my new title?"

I am not going to present a laundry list of clients, partly because they are far too numerous, and partly because I wish to preserve their privacy. (What was said to me behind closed doors, remains behind closed doors!) But many who hired me to help *them* ended up becoming *my* mentors. You know who you are. Working with you has been a privilege, not to mention a barrel of fun.

So the list below—partial by default—represents my heartfelt thanks to those who have mentored me, consciously or unconsciously:

Sue Collier, publisher and coach, who besides knowing her craft, sees the world through similar eyes. Elizabeth Lesser, whose own work I so admire and who became the voice in my head holding up the standard of excellence in writing. And finally, friends and colleagues whose lives have touched mine and whose voices have inspired me:

Ananda Apfelbaum, Lia Aprile, Laura Beck, Rafael Bejarano, Steve Bodkin, Lisa Cameron, Pana Della Valle, Sally Hunt, Linda Jame, Susan & Shaun Johnston, Stass Klassen, Carole Sue Lipman, Rich MacDonald, Barbara Perlmutter, Nuria Pujol Valls, Margo Saltz, Karen & Len Schifrin, Arje & Esther Shaw, Michelle Shaw, Lisa Sulgit, Leah Washington, Linda Woznicki.

Much of this book deals with seeking inspiration within. But connecting with kindred spirits helps validate what we find within—for here, as in all things, the Law of Attraction is at work…and at play.

He who knows others
is learned;
He who knows himself
is wise.

—Lao-Tzu

I.
THE BUILDING BLOCKS

Introduction

W hen are you going to write a book about your work?" my playwright friend and client, Rich, kept asking.

"Never! I'm not going to write a book about public speaking. It's all been said and done already."

"No, not the way you do it. You *know* you're going to write a book, so why don't you get started?"

I heartily disagreed. I did not want to write about my work unless I felt I was adding a new way of looking, a different approach, a new insight. I knew deep inside I was getting results from people that surprised me—and surprised even them. But I was not sure *how* my coaching produced the results it did. Above all, I could not figure out how it could be explained.

So our little dialogue went on for years. And finally Rich wore me out!

It took me many years of coaching my clients to *feel* that my approach was, indeed, different. But I still could not figure out how to turn a feeling into a *telling*.

Then, suddenly (after twenty-four years), I was ready.

I was ready when it occurred to me that *what* I was doing was not so unique, but my *approach* was. I have always been more interested in the spiritual aspect of my clients, in what goes on inside, which, I invariably knew, would be what showed up outside in their performance. And by cultivating their inner world, we are able to tap into their truest part.

I was ready when I realized that listening was as integral to communicating as was speaking; that by listening for what was not being said, I could help them clarify what was. I was ready when I saw that who we are in private would inevitably be who we are in public (speaking and life). That hiding behind a façade or a slide show was hiding our light. And that *the public was far more interested in our light than in our words.*

I was ready when I realized that the fear of public speaking is a spiritual malady and must be met on spiritual grounds if we are to deal with it at all. This means that *preparation must start with the speaker—not with the speech.* It means that the mechanics of crafting a talk must take second place to the inward reflection that gives a speaker true confidence.

And so this slim volume, I hope, will make you aware of what the true building blocks are that go into speaking, into uncovering the essence of who you are and what you have to say. *It is meant not only for those who must speak before large groups; it will be helpful in all situations where an open heart and truthful words are your goal.*

Who Should Read This?

You should read this. Even if you don't consider your-self a public speaker, you need this book. The fact is that everyone—from homemakers to lawmakers, from leaders to leading ladies, from talking heads to corporate heads—will at one time or another have to stand up and be heard.

If you don't know how to relax in front of an audience, you need this book. If you dread the thought of revealing yourself, you need this book. It will convince you that you have what it takes...that the answers are within you...that your job is one of discovery rather than mastery.

When you discover your passion, you will master the art of speaking. When you find your voice, you'll be able to give voice to your vision.

Granted, public speaking may be your worst nightmare. You're not alone.

Jerry Seinfeld, commenting on the fact that the fear of pub-lic speaking trumps the fear of death, points out that if you had to attend a funeral, you'd rather be the guy *in* the casket than the one delivering the eulogy!

But public speaking can no longer be avoided—no matter what your career. And there is no reason to avoid it, for, in fact, we all do it every day. Whenever you open your mouth to speak, you *are* speaking in public (unless you are in a closet muttering to yourself). We don't, of course, regard our daily discourse as public speaking. But I maintain that if you can speak to one, you can speak to one hundred.

The difference between talking to a friend and talking to a group lies not in the number of people confronting you but in how you confront yourself: how you feel about being seen and heard; how you approach the task. The way you affect an audience stems from the way you first affect yourself. Do you panic at the thought of getting up? Do you take the time to prepare? Does your preparation include thinking about your audience? Do you listen well? Do you listen at all? The answers to these questions will give you a signal as to how others will perceive you.

After working with speakers of all stripes, I have seen people change from boring to sparkling—not because I waved a magic wand over them but because they found their own voice.

Finding your own voice may take two hours or two months. It depends on how deeply it is buried. But know that it is there. In fact, everything you need to become a riveting public speaker is already inside. My job as a coach is to dig with you, much the way that Michelangelo chipped away at the stone he claimed was hiding the figures embedded within.

In the course of my digging, I have unearthed some of life's lessons. They may have originated in public speaking but they have as much to say about how we live as about how we speak.

What Is This Book About?

This is and isn't a book about speaking in public. It is, rather, a book about *awareness*— the awareness that every time you open your mouth to say anything, you *are* speaking in public. And if you can speak to one, surely, you can speak to two; if you can speak to two, you can speak to three. Just keep adding, and soon you will see that when you have found your voice, it does not matter how many people are listening.

This book is also about the awareness that what you put forth is what you will get back; the awareness that you can't be someone on stage that you are not off stage; that how you listen will determine how you are perceived as a speaker.

This book is about the awareness that success is secondary to significance. If your heart is open and your intentions clear, *success will find you as you seek significance.* Care less about the outcome and more about your actions. The outcome will take care of itself if you take care of your choices.

But most of all, this book is about becoming aware of your own voice. This means going within, for that is where your own true voice is to be found. You will not find it in books, nor in seminars. *You will not find your voice in how others see you, but in how you see yourself.*

This book will make you aware that *facts and figures don't persuade. Passion does!* Discovering your passion is intimately linked to finding your voice. They feed each other. They live side by side.

When you craft a talk about which you are passionate, you become the expert; you become the leader. If your notes were to blow away, you would not be derailed for the story would still be within you. And for a story to be arresting, it must derive from your insights—yours and yours alone. No one else creates your point of view. And no one else speaks in your voice.

When you know what is important to you, what values you hold dear, what your purpose is, you sparkle. No one can sparkle for you. Sparkle comes from within. So does conviction; so, too, confidence.

Confidence can be learned—but not from a book. Confidence comes from living. It comes from absorbing life's lessons and from being tested by life's obstacles. Certainly, much has been written about confidence—how to get it, how to project it, how to act it. But know this: You cannot apply confidence as if it were makeup; you cannot treat it as a shield to hide your flaws.

Either you own it, or you don't. You can't fake it, make it, or break it. You can, however, become aware of your negative thinking, get out of the way, and allow yourself to *transform your fear into your forte.* Allowing is so very different from forcing. It is also the key to your success. Why is this so?

The more you force something, the more you battle with it. Here, the battle is internal, which means that a part of you must lose for another part of you to win. This, in turn, means that one part of you is always having to suppress another. And the more you suppress something, the more it eventually shows up elsewhere. *We can't rid ourselves of what we suppress.* We will always be subservient to it until we meet it head on. Keep in mind that battling involves resistance; there is no battle when your opponent simply steps aside. So when your ego steps aside, when your fears are distracted by your engagement in something that gives you joy, there is no need for battle.

When you *allow* your fears to drop away, you stop doing battle. You acknowledge the fears, and you move ahead despite them. You put your attention elsewhere. You relax into knowing what you know. Then you don't have to fake anything. You are at peace and at home within yourself. That is the true definition of confidence.

When it comes to public speaking, *fear is a spiritual malady.* It's not the same as coming face-to-face with a snake or with someone who's pointing a gun at you. The fear of speaking before others originates in your imagination—not in your reality. It must, therefore, be dealt with on a spiritual plane. All the pointers, tips, and tricks in the world—helpful though they may be—will not quell your fears if you don't find peace within, where these fears originate.

This book, then, is not a formula for success in public speaking. Others have tackled that subject. *This book is a guide to understanding your own outlook.* How you look at the world will determine how the world looks at you—both on the podium and off. And once you commit to looking within before you speak, others can't help but notice the power of your vision and the passion in your voice.

> *"I am an old man and have known*
> *many troubles, but most of them*
> *never happened."*
> —Mark Twain

*"Begin each day's journey
with a ten-minute walk
within your soul."*
—*It's the Thought That Counts*

The Secret to Public Speaking

It is going to surprise—if not shock—you. Not because it is so strange but because it is so common. It is not something that has been hiding in a cave. It is not esoteric, though few would necessarily connect it with public speaking. It is free and requires no learning, although it does require, perhaps, a change of habit.

It is both mysterious and obvious. It is not taught in school, but teachers love it. It belongs to us all, from birth to death, and we all engage it at critical moments. It is a paradox when coupled with speaking, but without it, speaking would be of no value. What you make of it is what it will return to you.

Are you ready to learn the secret? It is *silence!*

How can silence be the great secret to public speaking?

Silence operates on two levels. Just as in music, there could be no notes without the silence that separates them, so too in speech, we need silence between words and thoughts. But that is the *use* of silence—vitally important, yet not the silence I am referring to here.

The silence of which I speak is the silence we experience

when we stop the merry-go-round of life; the silence of meditation, of contemplation, of going within to that quiet place where we turn off the world and listen to the cosmos. The silence that brings us in touch with what really matters, with what we most dearly intend. This place of silence is where clarity resides; it is where confidence is born.

The silence of which I speak is not the same as sitting still and thinking. Thought can turn into rumination; ruminations can turn into worry; worry can turn into fear; and fear can turn into paralysis. These activities never promote confidence.

No, the silence of which I speak is the silence where *thought* ends and *being* begins. The place where you simply are; the place of no thought, no worry, no fear; the place where you listen to your heart, or your highest Self. Of course, thought has its place, but not here—not in silence. Thought must be put on hold for the moment.

If we wish to speak well in public, we would be best served to spend time in silence, for without it, we will be making noise and not sense. It is paradoxical, but true: Before you can shine as a speaker, you must spend time being quiet. The most private part of you must inform the most public part. Anything less is busywork.

Preparation, organization, practice…all are vital…all have a place before you take your place on stage. But *if you have not spent time in silence, you will be busy without really knowing why.*

> *"Experience will guide us to
> the rules," he said.
> You cannot make rules precede
> practical experience."*
> —Antoine de St. Exupery

"The Silent Way"

Silence has dominated my teaching and coaching career for thirty years.

While still a babe in the woods professionally, I was sent to study an innovative approach to education devised by Dr. Caleb Gattegno, former colleague of Dr. Jean Piaget, the well-known Swiss child psychologist. Dr. G., as we called him, was a believer in silence. Indeed, he founded his institute, Educational Solutions, on it. A renaissance man—fluent in many languages, in Eastern philosophy, in psychology, math, and reading—Dr. Gattegno was courageous enough to take a hard look at what was happening—and not happening—in our schools.

What he observed in the language classroom was obvious but unnoticed until then: that the teacher—the one who already spoke the language—was also the one getting the most practice at it. The students were not using the language half as much as the teacher was modeling it. This seemed backwards to him, so he set out to change it.

In his approach, called the Silent Way, the teacher remains silent and the students discover how the language works. "How is this possible?" I wondered, as you may be wondering too.

Dr. Gattegno believed in play as the creative force in learning. So he devised a series of games using a set of colored rods, which the teacher manipulates. The teacher models each word only once and allows the students to play with them. By stringing together the words without ever being told how, the students discover the rules of the language *on their own*. They are never given rules; they help *create* them through silent corrections. They play with pronunciation; they play with structure. And because the teacher is not constantly modeling, they are forced to listen well, just as the teacher is forced to listen well for the correct models among the students.

In the Silent Way classroom, there are no exams and no tests of any kind; they are unnecessary. Since every utterance gives the teacher an idea of where the student is and what he has yet to figure out, each person's progress is always evident. The real work is in creating teachers with the talent to listen well, observe accurately, and be patient.

One of the most telling experiences I had with this approach came early in my career of teaching English as a Second Language. I had a large class of about thirty adults. We had been together for more than six months and were working on a complex structure for a beginning group. It entailed the distinction between a real event and a hypothetical event and how the verbs differ in each. For instance: "If I *give* you $7, *will* you buy me lunch?" (A real event) versus "If I *gave* you $500, what *would* you do with it?" (A hypothetical event)

The students were playing with these options and calling out answers. They were getting close, but none of them had gotten it right.

Sitting at my right was a painfully shy young woman. I could not get her to open her mouth despite the fact that she came to every class, paid close attention, smiled and laughed a lot, and seemed to be taking it all in. I don't know if she had said more than five words in six months, and although I encouraged her, she just would not participate. After many weeks of this, I just let her be. I figured that the most important thing was for her to be present and be enjoying the interactions.

Suddenly, in a moment of relative quiet, she called out the perfect sentence, structure intact, and all the verbs in the right tense. Every one looked at her with amazement and admiration. It was a jaw-dropping moment. She sat there beaming as the group broke out into spontaneous applause.

It was a moment I shall never forget, for it taught me that of all the virtues, patience is vital. There's no accounting for the speed at which people absorb information, nor does silence indicate that someone is not working hard.

In some ways, a Silent Way classroom resembles a pantomime show, with everyone having a good time. The results are nothing short of amazing. Although this is not the place to delve deeply into this approach, suffice it to say that it most closely mirrors the way that children teach themselves their native tongue—most by the age of three or four.

■ ■ ■ ■ ■

The Silent Way formed the foundation of my work, long after I left the language classroom. What I learned, above all, was that we don't learn from others. *Anything of value, we teach ourselves.* Our mentors serve only as catalysts. If we are not ready to learn, no teacher can reach us; and when we are ready, no one can stop us. Above all, learning is a joy, not a chore. When you remove judgment—right and wrong—and focus on the task at hand, people automatically relax and join in the fun.

This type of teaching was great fun for both teacher and student, and a far cry from the rigorous discipline of my own education. I became determined to carry this sense of fun and exploration into my consulting career and my work as a coach. I figured that if I was going to spend most of my day doing something, I had better enjoy it.

The Silent Way was a gift to me at the outset of my career. Little did I know how it would influence my entire life. It taught me the value of listening. It taught me that silence is the bedrock of creativity; it is where we go when we want to understand anything of importance—including who we are, and why we are here. When you delve into your own deep well of silence, you too will come to the source of your own creativity, your own power, and your own voice.

The Second Secret to Public Speaking

Silence, as fundamental as it is, is not enough. Obviously, you can use silence in speaking, but you can't *be* silent *while* speaking. So, there is a *second secret* to public speaking, and it too is no mystery. It too is with us from our earliest days to our last. It too is omnipresent. We rely on it to guide us, entertain us, intrigue us, move us, and inspire us. It will make us laugh, cry, think, and feel every emotion we are capable of feeling. What is it?

It is *story!*

Stories are part of life. They reflect how we see the world; how we see each other; how we see ourselves. A good story will cut through reams of facts, figures, and falsehoods. A good story will be remembered—without notes. It will be quoted. It will enlighten. It will inspire.

A public speaker without a story will be of no interest for a very simple reason: We won't remember what was said—not in the long run. For *we cannot retain isolated facts, figures, or features of a speech unless they are couched in story.* Lists of bullet points turn to mush in our brain. Words start swimming away. Thoughts fade. We learn information through story. So our job is to convey that story to others, making it as visual as possible.

Developing a good story is a personal journey. You must dig deep to find your truth. A coach can help. An objective listener can help. But know that you need to practice with someone who is not afraid to tell you the truth.

If you are a powerful executive who can cause heads to roll, you may not be hearing the truth from those in your employ. If you are practicing before those who have anything at stake (such as their jobs), they may not even know the truth.

The real truth resides within. That is why *silence* and *story* go hand-in-hand. They are the two bookends that support you as speaker. The secrets are simple. Putting them into practice is where the work begins. So let's begin!

The Law of Attraction: What You See Is What You Get

Imagine how different we would feel if we deliberately created our life rather than just reacted to it; if we chose our thoughts, rather than let our thoughts choose us; if we could see that what lives inside us is what we live on the outside. And that by changing what's inside, we change what we experience in the world outside.

The Law of Attraction teaches that like attracts like. It teaches that since we are all made up of energy, we vibrate at a certain frequency, just as a tuning fork does…just as every element in the universe does, including our thoughts. And through our thoughts, we attract similar thoughts, similar wavelengths, similar feelings.

I was first exposed to this way of thinking through the teachings of Abraham-Hicks in the late 1990s. (See www.abraham-hicks.com.) One crucial insight I gained from them is that *you can't feel two opposing emotions simultaneously.* This means that if you are feeling fear, you can't be feeling love *at the same moment.* If you are feeling joy, you can't be feeling fear. If you are feeling confident, you can't be feeling fretful. If you are feeling anxious, you can't be feeling delight. As Abraham points out, "A mother can't love *and* worry about her child at the same moment." I thought about that a lot. The mother may think she can hold opposing emotions at once, but the child feels the worry stronger than the love.

The reason for this is clear: An emotion that is totally positive cannot coexist with one that is totally negative. They may alternate, but they cannot occupy the same moment.

Not only is everyone and everything made up of vibrational energy (as quantum physics concludes), but the strong magnetic force of our vibration will ensure that when we are feeling negative, we attract negative thoughts and negative people. So too, when we feel positive, we attract the same. In other words, what you send out is what you get back. This applies to public speaking as to every other part of life. Furthermore, as Abraham teaches, we cannot vibrate for anyone else, nor can anyone vibrate for us. So the blame game is irrelevant. We get to own our own thoughts and our own behavior.

This understanding can be enormously liberating. It casts responsibility squarely on our own shoulders for what we emit, what we transmit, and what we receive. And by accepting responsibility, we gain the power to influence what comes to us and how we feel. Imagine the implications: No one else can ruin our day; no one else can hurt our feelings. We can *allow* a bad day; we can *allow* hurt feelings. But it is our choice! This does not mean that others won't get in our way, or annoy us completely. But we can choose to walk away or accept these behaviors and other people having a bad day, and not make it our own.

With this awareness, we understand our role in speaking (as in life). If we exude fear and dread on the podium, we will experience negative energy coming back to us.

If we exude pleasure and passion, we will receive the same. Returning to silence, if we spend time in meditation, we can achieve clarity about who we are, what we stand for, what we value, and what ignites us. And when we achieve clarity, we know just what we want to say…in public, in private, in all of life.

The best preparation is to go within. Sit quietly; do yoga; take a walk in the woods or in a park; take a leisurely bath. Do what you must to slow down. Give yourself the luxury of peace and quiet *on a regular basis*. There you will meet your best self— the part of you that knows exactly what you want to say and why. There you will find your purpose. *There you will not be concerned with success: there you will find significance.*

The silence in which you allow yourself to steep will reward you many times over for it is the source of all that is real within you. It is the place where clarity resides.

"Your actions are a portrait
of your soul."
—It's the Thought That Counts

Vision + Values = Voice

Woven throughout this book is the notion that to succeed in public speaking, we must find our own unique voice. But where does this voice originate? How do we discover it?

Our voice derives from two primary sources: our vision of the world and our personal values. These may change over time, but in any given moment, our vision and values give rise to our voice.

By vision, I do not mean a specific goal, as in a corporate vision. Here, I use vision to describe how we see the world...how we think it operates. Is it a hostile place where we must vigilantly defend what is ours? Is it a hospitable place where we move outward from security and trust; a belief that all will work out for the best, no matter what the path?

Do we see the world as driven by competition, or do we see it as fueled by creativity? Is it a zero-sum game, where if you win, I lose; or is it a spring from which the more we take, the more there is to be taken? Is it a place of lack or a place of abundance? Is it a universe with renewable resources or diminishing returns? Is it a place for survival of the fittest, or are we all fit to survive—given the proper resources? Does compassion underlie our outlook or does competition rule? Can we afford to trust or must we control?

Our answers to these questions will tell us about our vision. But know that our answers are not necessarily fixed. They need not be written in stone. For these are beliefs. And belief systems can change—with volition. If we wish to change them, we can. But we have to be willing and ready. If you've ever tried to argue anyone out of a belief that was held dearly, you know how immovable they are (both the beliefs and the people). But sometimes life itself proves our beliefs to be wrong, or at least unworkable. Then we are ripe for change. A bumper sticker I once saw admonishes: "Don't always believe what you think!"

Intimately tied to our vision are our values. Our values tell us what we believe because we act them out every day. *Our values come not from what we claim but from what we do,* from our behaviors.

The man who tells you his family comes first and then spends most evenings and weekends at the office; carries a beeper, cell phone, and Blackberry; and who is seldom *present* while at home is not *living* the values he speaks.

The woman who is looking for love and then proceeds to enumerate a laundry list of why all men are cads—unreliable, uncaring, ungiving, and incomprehensible—is not likely to find the love she craves, primarily because she doesn't believe it is available.

Our values are evident to all who know us. But they are often least evident to ourselves. Why is this? It is because what we proclaim with our mouth is not always how we conduct our lives. Here again, the Law of Attraction is at work. If we hold that all men are skunks, we are not going to come upon roses. If we claim that we value something, and then place it on the backburner of our lives, we are not being true to our words.

When we finally live our values, when we finally gain clarity of vision, then—and only then—do we uncover our voice. For our voice cannot be authentic until it is integrated with our values, resting firmly on our vision. And *an inauthentic voice is what sends us to the podium short of breath and with knocking knees.*

Voice derives from the truest part of who we are. It cannot be learned; it can only be discovered. It is always there, although at times it is buried. We just have to quiet down and listen. Silence is the soil in which our true voice thrives. It is there that we find the space to look at how we live, not merely at what we say.

■ ■ ■ ■ ■

Consider these two stories about two women, both of them actresses, both of them friends. The life of an actress in New York is not the stuff of glamour that many assume. It is filled with rejection, struggle, hunger, and heartache—and that includes the fortunate ones who are working!

The first actress is a seasoned veteran of staggering talent. She has been acting for more than thirty years, on Broadway, Off-Broadway, and everywhere in between. Like most in her profession, she has had periods of plenty and periods of empty. She has known standing ovations as well as casting directors who would barely glance up from their sandwiches as she auditioned. Her career has been in turmoil because an actress over age fifty is not a valued commodity in the United States. The truth of this is commonly accepted. My friend has felt the brunt of this so often, it has bruised her to her core.

She has taken her personal value from those others have placed on her. And her pain is palpable.

Only when she is working is she happy. Only when she is on stage does her sense of self thrive. She has so confused her personal worth with her theatrical worth that when she speaks (without a script), she rushes through her words as if we will all run away to more important things before she can finish her sentence. Her friends and husband adore her, but until she is able to love herself, her voice will be stunted because of her self-limiting values.

The second actress is young and very committed to personal growth and to her burgeoning career. She has wanted to act since she was nine years old. With this clear vision for her life, she went to drama school, came to NYC to "make it," and has taken every role that has been offered to gain experience. (What young actor, after all, can afford to turn anything down?) As a result, she has acted in work that she did not believe in, which placed her out of her own integrity. And after several years, she has begun to doubt her acting chops—losing confidence just when she should be gaining it. All this became obvious when I asked her the following question:

"Do you think you can act as well in a character that you don't relate to as in one that you do?"

Epiphany! She realized that her heart was not in many of the roles she had taken. No wonder she felt depleted by these roles rather than enriched by the experience. The fact is that whenever we force ourselves into a "should," "ought to," or "must" situation, it comes back to bite us in the ass!

It may not always be possible to do what we want, simply because we do not always know what we want. But when we start listening to our own true voice, and then deny or reject it, we are *choosing* suffering over joy. When this talented young woman figures out that her vision and her values are choices, she will regain her voice (which stems from integrity) and say "No," when she can, and "Yes," when she wants to.

If you are thinking, "Yes, but we can't always make the choice we truly want," I concede that this is sometimes true. But the choice that we *always* have is this:

We may not be able to control all conditions outside of ourselves, but we can always control the conditions inside of ourselves. We can change our attitude, if not the event. We can change our view, if not the reality.

Eastern philosophies teach us that there is no reality—just

perception. And we get to choose how we perceive events, situations, conditions and people who come into our lives, sometimes unbidden. If we choose to see a public speaking engagement as an event upon which to dump our worst fears, that will become a self-fulfilling prophecy; so too, if we see it as an opportunity to display our strengths, that becomes our reality.

The difference between a
stepping stone and a
stumbling block is in
the way you approach it.

Confidence: What It Is...What It Isn't

I don't know anyone who wouldn't want to feel more confident in front of a group. I also know that those I've worked with invariably do end up feeling vastly more confident. But I never *work* on confidence. Never! The reason is simple: *Confidence is a byproduct of doing what you enjoy. Never does it stand alone.*

Confidence always derives from content. It must! It may be the content of your talk, of your thinking, feeling, self-talk, self-esteem. If you are not at home in your own skin, then confidence will be nothing more than a pose, a posture. But if you like yourself, if you feel passion for your topic, if you simply can't wait to get up and speak, and if you approach your audience with respect, then you will exude confidence.

Confidence alone can't be practiced, nor can it be programmed. But the content of your talk can be. When you have practiced enough, when you really enjoy your message, when you have tailored it to be not too long and not too cryptic, then confidence appears without your having to chase it.

If anything you say on the podium is at odds with who you are inside, even the most confident of stances will not ring true. Confidence is not a mask you hide behind. It is a gift you give yourself and your audience when your story comes from the heart.

One more ingredient: Your story must be fun. If it's not fun to tell, how can it be fun to hear? I'm not saying funny; I am saying you must take pleasure in telling your tale.

Some messages are not fun, nor are they meant to be. No matter. It is enough to be in the limelight because you believe that *what you have to say is worth hearing.*

■ ■ ■ ■ ■

Sometimes arrogance is mistaken for confidence. The two should not be confused. Confidence puts people at ease; arrogance puts people off.

The overly confident may appear arrogant. But I've learned that true confidence grows out of security; arrogance, from insecurity. It may seem like there is a fine line dividing the two, whereas, in reality, they are polar opposites. Suffice it to say if you can be both confident and humble, you will be perceived well. (The two are a paradox but not mutually exclusive.) If you speak from your own truth, you will feel confident. And you will be humble if you understand that yours is not the *only* truth. But know that confidence bordering on condescension will cause you to be perceived badly. (No one wants to feel inferior to you.)

Your own outlook is crucial. Again, *how you look at the world will reflect how the world looks at you.*

"Some people don't communicate.
They just take turns talking."
—It's the Thought That Counts

Do You Have Three Legs?
What All Speakers Must Share

Stories abound. So do storytellers. Many years ago, I had the task of figuring out what common traits all good public speakers shared—in other words, my philosophy of public speaking. At the time, like most others, I could recognize a great speaker when I heard one, but I didn't see what linked them or even if they were linked at all. But upon examination, I came to see that they do share three traits. And so was born my three-legged philosophy. These three legs, like the legs of a stool, must all be present for success in speaking. Otherwise you topple over. Let me illustrate them with the following scenarios:

—A brilliant teacher is at the podium. He has been teaching undergraduates for twenty years, and for many of those years has gotten rave reviews along the grapevine. He is knowledgeable, his material is well-organized. You take copious notes but are terribly bored. Why? Because he has been doing the same thing for two decades years and is stale. He has lost his enthusiasm, and therefore, so do you.

—A company scandal makes headlines. The PR executive in charge of damage control is sent to the local TV station for an interview. He is savvy but not convincing. He knows, in his heart of hearts, that something is amiss (and that it will probably be exposed as the investigation deepens). You don't believe what he is saying because *he* doesn't believe what he is saying. He's a hired gun, and it shows. It sneaks out not in his words but in his body language; in the way he doesn't meet the eye of the reporter or the camera. It comes out in the lack of spontaneity and sincerity. (Many executives these days get media training, but what they forget is that their audiences have watched enough media events to know when someone is covering up.)

—A young executive has just been named president of a company. He is eager, charming, and sincere. He wants to do well. But he doesn't know how to do right. Over time, people lose confidence in his judgment and start ignoring his counsel. Why? He doesn't know the business and believes that managing means organizing things. He has yet to learn that it really means directing people so they get the best out of themselves.

So exactly what are these three legs? They are:
1. Expertise
2. Enthusiasm
3. Credibility

EXPERTISE: How well do you know your stuff? Are you faking it? Are you comfortable in your knowledge?
or
Are you skimming the surface, hoping that no one will ask an in-depth question? Are you afraid to listen?

ENTHUSIASM: Are you passionate about your message?

Do you have a purpose that excites you? Do you really care? Does the subject still interest you?

or

Are you burned out? Have you heard it all before? Has your spark fizzled?

CREDIBILITY: Are you telling the truth? Do you believe your story in your heart?

or

Are you spouting company policy because you are on salary? Are you speaking from personal integrity?

It pays to be brutally honest with yourself when answering these questions because these attitudes seep out through your body language as well as your words. You may think you can control your words, but your body language will give you away—even with media training!

So what should you do when you are not as expert as you'd like to be...not as enthused as you wish you were...not as convinced as you'd prefer?

Tell the truth!

Say, "The story I am here to tell is something that I have just learned. I am not an expert but am most eager to share with you what I do know."

Say, "The results of this research are still coming in, and the preliminary findings have surprised even us. I can't yet vouch for their accuracy, but I can report them as is."

Say, "I have my doubts about these facts, but I'll keep you abreast of news as it occurs."

There is nothing wrong with saying, "I don't know." But there's plenty wrong with pretense. The audience may not know your topic, but they can smell a phony from a distance.

■ ■ ■ ■ ■

My three-legged philosophy was born at the outset of my career. And it is as true today as it was more than twenty-five years ago—with one difference: It has become more nuanced.

People mature over time, and with them their philosophies. Today, I see the subtleties as well as the surface. Today, I see that what accounts for a good speaker is far larger than the sum of these three parts.

Today, I see that passion, mandatory still, does not always look like passion. It doesn't always flaunt itself. It may take the form of a quiet knowing…a certainty that can't be shaken and does not have to be proven…an inner calm that resembles passion less, and presence more.

Today, I appreciate presence, though defining it is nearly impossible. I have spent countless hours, and many an enjoyable dinner, discussing presence and what it looks like. To no avail. It is something we *feel* rather than describe. It is something as intangible— and potent—as love. I see it as a connection to our own divinity. When you meet someone who has presence, you simply know it. It is there, but it doesn't shout. It simply is. Presence is not something you strive to achieve. It is a gift. I know we all have this gift. We just have to let it come forth without manipulation, without chasing it. It is synonymous with charisma. And just as elusive. It is a magnetic force that will show itself when we are true to our most genuine self, when we speak in our voice from the depth of our knowing.

Today, I see credibility as a constant. It, too, is not something for which you strive. You either believe every word you utter, or you don't. It is what children intuit when sizing up an adult. It changes not with circumstances; it is tied not to political correctness, nor to popularity. It is not an "on again, off again" quality. It hits no false notes. It is born of integrity.

I see integrity as the sum of a good speaker. It comes from within.

It does not ebb and flow. It releases the speaker from fear because her every word rings true. It relaxes the listener because he knows he is in good hands. When we operate from our integrity, we wear the mantle of confidence without even trying. We are ourselves—our best selves. We speak with authority—an authority that cannot be shaken. We look people in the eye, and they feel the connection; we look them in the eye and they feel understood, even if we don't say a word.

Nothing can replace integrity: no tips, no tricks, no amount of practice can make up for what you have not uncovered at your core. *Without integrity, nothing you say will carry much weight. With it, you cannot fail.*

> *"The difference between genius
> and stupidity is that genius has its limits."*
> —Albert Einstein

The Clever vs. the Wise

Throughout my career, I have been privileged to work with brilliant people. What surprised me at first was that the truly brilliant minds want to share what they know and are so comfortable in themselves that they can leave their egos aside. Whereas those who are just clever, or insecure, need to show off.

I've also observed the almost-brilliant—the wannabe geniuses. They mistake "smarts" for knowledge. They will sometimes appear condescending to their audience. A speaker who talks down to his audience is terribly misguided. Naturally, we all want to look smart at the front of a room. But we'd be much smarter if we spent time helping our audience feel smart rather than showing off our own knowledge.

The best of the best don't worry about appearing smart. They've already nailed being smart. So what they reveal to their audience is their humanity. And it wins the crowd each and every time. If you have any doubts, consider which of these two remarks *you* would rather hear at the end of your speech:

"He seemed to know his stuff, but I didn't understand a word!"

or

"She was amazing! She took such a complex topic and made it so clear!"

This suggests the conundrum: *Are those at the top of their game there because they know more, or are they always seeking to know more, which puts them at the top of their game?*

"Don't expect people to look up to you if you look down on them."

On a Personal Note

When I began coaching public speakers in 1980, I knew nothing about the field. If anyone had told me I'd have a thriving career coaching Ph.D. expert witnesses in major court battles, I would have thought they were nuts. If anyone had told me I'd be working with CEOs and top litigators, I would have laughed!

At that time, I was known in my field of educational consulting as a creative teacher working with the Silent Way and was invited to demonstrate this new technique in universities, at language schools and at international conferences. I had under my belt: seven years in the college classroom, two years training executives in corporate America, three years of specialized training with Dr. Gattegno, an M.A. degree from Columbia University, and a good deal of bravado.

Bravado, I know, can sound like empty puffery. But in this case, it came from having just lived through seven of the toughest teaching years of my life. And I figured if I could succeed at that, then anything else would seem like child's play.

I certainly did not perceive myself as a public speaker— despite the many occasions I had stood in front of a large room giving demonstrations and leading discussions. And thank God for that! For if I had considered what I was doing to be (public enemy #1) public speaking, I would have been as intimidated as the next person, and probably would have spent an inordinate amount of energy trying to get out of it.

But I spoke in front of large and small groups unselfconsciously because I was sharing information I was passionate about. I was sharing material that was a lot of fun to demonstrate. I just knew they'd love it, and they did. And part of my mission was to change education as I had known it into an experience where having a great time and learning could happily coexist.

■ ■ ■ ■ ■

So how did I get myself into this unlikely career?

It was in response to a job offer—one I promptly turned down the minute I heard it was to work with Ph.D. economists who had to testify in court as expert witnesses. My reasons seemed sound at the time. I figured that since I had assiduously avoided taking Econ101 through four years of college and then graduate school, I was not suited for the job. What's more, I had never taken an hour's worth of public speaking, so I assumed that my credentials were not up to par. But I decided at least to talk to the president of the firm and find out what he wanted. That decision was to change the course of my life, creating a career I couldn't possibly have dreamt of because I didn't even know it existed! And, in fact, it is a career that I helped to create.

As it turned out, this president was actually looking for someone with my liberal arts background who was *not* familiar with economic terms. He was delighted that I knew nothing of experts, juries, courtroom procedures, depositions, or economic models. I thought that only kings were "deposed," and all "models" had long legs and perfect bodies.

At that time, I had been running my own consulting business called Plain English, Please!—helping businesses drop their jargon in favor of real communication. And that is exactly what he was looking for.

But the real reason I was hired, I believe, had little to do with credentials or even experience. It had to do with "chemistry." The kind that makes people "click." I really hit it off with the president and his top staff. And I learned that day that *we are not always hired for what we know; we are sometimes hired for our know-how.* I may not have known economics, but I did know how to talk to people, how to listen to them, and how to gain their trust. I always saw my work with them as a partnership. They taught me economics; I taught them how to put it into plain English. It's hard to say who learned more. I was tutored by the best, and I gave them my best.

It was a relationship that was to last for twenty years. The referrals alone kept my coaching business thriving with no marketing, no advertising—only word-of-mouth. It brought me into the boardrooms and the courtrooms of America to help experts articulate complex issues in simple language. And it all happened because I took a chance on something new, and a man with foresight took a chance on me.

I learned on the job, and the job expanded as I learned how to do it. As corporate events grabbed the headlines, CEOs had to hone their speaking skills. As anti-trust cases captured the spotlight, expert testimony could make the difference between winning or losing millions.

One of the many challenges for an expert witness is the audience he must face. It may be either a dazed jury being asked to weigh and sift confusing or conflicting evidence; or an overburdened judge who would like to cut through the thicket of words and get to the point.

In either case, the job of the expert is to help them make sense of it all. Often, buckets of money are at stake, and the expert has to boil down months of research, truckloads of reports, and mountains of data into a coherent and authoritative story. And a story it must be. For without a story the details would cloud the issues.

■ ■ ■ ■ ■

Enron as Morality Tale

As an example, let's look at one of the major corporate criminal trials to date in America, the Enron scandal. The prosecution had the daunting task of trying to explain accounting fraud to a jury: a sure recipe for boredom if ever there was one! And they knew it. Wisely, they did not make the *details* of Enron's actions the theme of their story.

Instead they framed the issue as: Telling the Truth vs. Telling Lies to the Marketplace. The dominant question became, "Did Enron manipulate the market?" That is a question we all can grasp. And the question bears repetition, as a theme, to lend cohesion to the myriad facts and nuances of the story. Piling up of facts or data can leave an audience behind in the dust in no time at all. *If you don't supply a story as structure, the jury has nothing to hang the facts on.* In the courtroom, as on the podium, as in life, story—along with expertise, sincerity, and credibility—is at the heart of success.

Lessons Learned

What I take away from my career is this: It matters not whether you are in the boardroom, the courtroom, the TV studio, or the conference room. It matters not whether you are at the top or the middle of the totem pole. What differentiates the gifted speaker from the crashing bore boils down, again, to finding your own voice. You must really know what you're talking about—not because you've read it in a book, but because you believe it in your heart. *You will never persuade others of what you don't first believe.*

You must not be afraid to show your passion. Many corporate leaders assume it is not professional to be passionate. But I ask you this: *If you don't passionately believe in what you're saying, why should we?*

Over the years, I've been privileged to make friends of many clients. So I've had occasion to see that finding their voice carries over into their personal lives. Who we are on stage carries over into who we are off stage.

When you speak your truth, you find meaning in your life—in the office, with friends, and at home.

When you find your passion, you enable and encourage others to do the same. What's more, you attract passionate people with passionate ideas to you. The Law of Attraction states that this is inevitable. If you wish to lead an organization with passionate people, set the tone. If you wish to have others engage fully, set the example. If you wish to have others care about you, care about them. As the adage reminds us, *People don't care how much you know until they know how much you care.*

The Quiet Side of Speaking

In my early years of learning the Silent Way at seminars led by Dr. Gattegno, I experienced for the first time in my overeducated life what true learning was all about.

Until that time, education for me meant memorizing information, taking tests, writing papers, and proceeding along a well-worn path of rituals designed to earn a degree. With Dr. G., none of that existed. We would sit around from Friday evening until Sunday evening discussing an idea, such as, "The only thing educable in man is his awareness."

Dr. G did not lecture. He did not give tests. He did not even seem to care if we agreed with him or with each other. He was like an eccentric man feeding pigeons in the park. He would throw out a tidbit and then—silently—sit back waiting for one of us to pick it up and dissect it. He was in no rush. He said little. He listened a lot and spoke only when we seemed to need guidance back to the topic. He would not let us take notes, making us leave our notebooks behind.

He used to say, "When you take notes instead of listening, the paper learns and you remain ignorant!"

"But what if we forget something?" we would protest.

"If you forget something, it wasn't that important to you in the first place. You weren't meant to remember it," he would counter. "Besides you have the rest of your life to learn it another time."

For the first time in my life, I was expected to figure things out on my own. There were no right answers. He was more interested in how we thought than in how we reiterated what others had thought.

At first, I found the whole experience confusing and frustrating. I wanted answers, explanations. None were forthcoming. But when I let my frustration fall away and gave myself over to the process, I learned in a completely new way, which would stay with me forever. *The freedom to think for oneself is the greatest gift of learning.* Anything less is parroting. (Dr. G. disapproved of the term "teacher trainer." He would say, "Training is for pigeons, not for people.")

Silence, a major guest at his seminars, meant allowing an idea to gestate, then chewing on it until the idea began to taste like something; then seasoning it, refining it, and when ready, swallowing it, making it our own. But above all, he would never expect us to swallow anything we hadn't *felt* the truth of. And he possessed an uncanny sense of when we were paying lip service to the truth and when we finally got it.

At the time, he was a mystery to me. Now, more than thirty years later, I have come to recognize the same ability in myself. I can't tell you exactly where it came from, but I believe it stems from my experience in listening.

I have since come to see that the way we listen…the way we converse with one another…the way we treat one another is at the heart of all speaking, both public and private. I have learned that *you are unlikely to succeed as a speaker if you do not do well as a listener.* Your talk will lack humanity if you do not reveal your own.

Listening is, indeed, another form of silence. It is the receptive side of being silent but still engaging with another (the yin side of the yang). Listening may look like a quiet activity, but the best listening is active. Not active because you are busy planning your response to what you've heard a small part of, but because you are busy taking in the feelings as well as the words. A good listener is not passive. A good listener is thoroughly engaged, though silent. And that engagement makes the silence rich with understanding. When you are *listened to* in this way, you feel complete. When you *are listening* in this way, you feel enriched.

II.
THE BASICS

"Are you listening to me?"
—Every wife to every husband
on the planet

Our Two Brains

There are two kinds of listening: listening with your ears and listening with your gut. The first processes words; the second processes truths. The first hears what is offered; the second, what is hidden.

We often assume a good communicator is one who *speaks* well. In fact, I believe it is more often one who *listens* well.

Speaking presumes connecting. And when speech does not derive from connection, it tends to be vague or irrelevant, self-indulgent or pompous. Speaking does not occur in a vacuum. And since connection *must* be the goal of all speakers, it would serve us well to listen as we speak. We must listen with our eyes as well as our ears; we must watch our audience as much as they are watching us.

As a coach, I spend a lot of time listening. I listen to what is *not* being said as much as to what is. This takes practice. It also takes trust—in my gut reaction, in reading body language, in sensing the tone of voice, and in what comes in through all the senses. Most of all, it means trusting my intuition. Listening with your gut is not something you learn in school. But you do learn it in the school of life. You learn to read mixed messages from parents, partial truths from teachers, hidden meanings from lovers, lack of sincerity from politicians.

And now science is weighing in, too. Scientists have discovered that in the womb, the same brain cells that go to make up the brain also go to form the gut. So we have a thinking gut as well as a thinking brain. Consider the ramifications. This means, literally, that brain cells are at work when we say: "I have a gut feeling," or "My gut is telling me to..." It is no surprise, therefore, when our language reflects conflict, as in, "My head says yes, but my gut says no."

Our head brain is a reasoning tool: the gut brain, a feeling tool. When they are in conflict, we would be best off to "go with our gut." Why? Because our gut is not subject to verbal manipulation or to the tyranny of logic. Our gut operates from a higher, holistic level of consciousness—one that connects us to the cosmos—while our brain is swayed by reason, language, thoughts, and beliefs put there by others.

If you want to find your own voice, the best place to look is in your gut! Going with your gut means being true to yourself. In the best of worlds, when we unite our gut and our brain, then we really know how to listen...how to speak...and how to live.

There's Nobody Out There But You

A story circulating on the Internet by that ubiquitous author, Anonymous, illustrates another aspect of listening. It's called, "Are You Listening to Your Echo?" It goes like this:

Want to know the secret to all life's mysteries? It does not come from the outside world because that is but an echo of your inner thoughts. Everything comes from within. It's all in this simple story.

A son and his father were walking in the mountains. Suddenly the son falls, hurts himself, and screams, "Ah!"

To his surprise, he hears a voice repeating his scream from somewhere in the mountain. "Ah!"

Curious, he yells: "Who are you?"

He receives the answer: "Who are you?"

Angered at the response, he screams: "Coward!"

He receives back: "Coward!"

He looks to his father and asks: "What's going on?"

The father smiles and says: "My son, pay attention."

And then he screams to the mountain: "I admire you."

The voice answers: "I admire you."

Again, the man screams: "You are a champion!"

The voice answers, "You are a champion!"

The boy is surprised but still does not understand. Then the father explains:" People call this an echo, but it is also an example of how life will give back everything you say or do."

Life is a mirror, an echo, a reflection of what we feel inside. We may not always be in touch with our vibration on a conscious level, but all we need to do is look at our life to see what we are sending out. Therefore, if you want more love in the world, create more love in your heart. If you hold onto grievances, they will hold on to you and keep you prisoner. I once heard Deepak Chopra refer to a line from *A Course in Miracles:* "Every decision is a choice between a grievance and a miracle." Why would you not choose the miracle?

Private Dialogue
vs. Public Monologue

I hope you can see that who you are when speaking in public will always reflect who you are in private. The public forum merely magnifies what you have inside and what you transmit in your daily encounters. This may be good news, or bad. If you are charming in daily discourse, you can be so on stage. All you need to learn is not to block your natural tendencies. But if you are dull and dreary in real life, you are not likely to be scintillating at the podium.

If I dig just a bit, with the help of my clients, I hardly ever find a truly dull person. (Only once did I know someone who was so boring that, in the words of another who worked with him, "You could fall asleep between the two syllables when he said, *Hello.*" But his problem turned out to be a lack of intonation in his voice. He was actually a very interesting guy; his speech pattern is all that needed work. Of course, one's speech pattern derives from a deeper source, but that's a discussion for another day).

And although I don't believe that people are truly dull, I have sat through many a dull lecture with a speaker who was too tense to reveal buried assets; too nervous to be enjoying herself;

and too much like a deer in the headlights to be able to relax himself, and therefore, the audience.

I maintain that if you are sincere in a private conversation, you can be so in a public one. If you are passionate in sharing your advice with a friend, you can be so in front of an audience. If you can present your expertise to a team of three, you can share it with a group of three hundred. I maintain that if you can connect to one, you can connect to many. The difference lies not in the quantity of people in the room but in the quality of your connection.

If you have any doubts, ask yourself these questions:

"When does a private dialogue turn into public speaking?"

"How many people have to be present for you to cross the line from private to public discourse?"

"Does it really depend on the number of people in the room?" And if not, "What does it depend on?"

"*Today my boss told me to just relax and be myself.*
I'm no fool—that's how I lost my last job!"
—After Dinner Speeches

When Does a Chat Turn Into a Speech?

I magine for a moment that you are sitting in a café near work. You and two friends are unwinding at the end of a day, discussing a new client you've just landed. A few more people from work stop by and join your table. You now number six. You are holding forth on why the client is a plum, on what lies in store, and what you see as the outcome.

Is this public speaking? Of course not. You're just relaxing and shooting the breeze with a group of colleagues.

Now imagine that four more people stop by your table and join the conversation. It has now moved from a cozy chat to a group of ten. Is it now public speaking? No, not yet.

But let's change the context just a bit. What if the president of your company asked you to talk to a different group of ten— the officers and board members? The subject remains the same— your new client, your mission, and the anticipated results. Is this public speaking? Yes, indeed.

What's the difference? When does a casual conversation become (the dreaded) public speaking?

When fear sets in!

When we worry more about how we're doing than about what we're saying, that's when we cross over. And fear comes in when we feel we are about to be judged. *Remove the judgment, and you remove the fear.*

Fear comes in when we add expectations: the expectation that we organize our thoughts, not just spout what comes to mind; the expectation that we be clear, authoritative, and eloquent. *Remove the expectation, and , again, you remove the fear.*

We cross the line, above all, when we are expected to perform.

At the café, you weren't performing for your friends; you were relaxing with them.

So consider that *performing takes place only in your mind.* If you don't perceive yourself as performing, it doesn't cripple you. Only when you become self-conscious does performance anxiety crush your natural exuberance. Performance anxiety, of course, afflicts not only speakers. It is the curse of all performing artists: dancers, musicians, singers, actors. The common denominator for all is *the fear of being judged.*

I've worked with highly skilled ballet dancers who never fear dancing in a rehearsal studio. But call it an audition, and performance anxiety sets in. It could even be the same room. The same music. The same combinations practiced over and over. But the mindset has changed: What once was fun becomes nerve-wracking.

Any speaker, singer, corporate chief, or actor will suffer from self-inflicted doubt once judgment gains the upper hand. But there is a simple solution that works every time.

"If you try to please the world,
you'll never please yourself."
—*It's the Thought That Counts*

Performance Anxiety

H ere's the good news: Performance anxiety will turn into performance joy *if you change the way you perceive your role.* As stated earlier, joy and fear cannot occupy the same vibration.

If you think you have to be perfect, you will tie yourself up in knots. If you simply expect to enjoy what you are doing, with no other agenda, no attachment to the outcome (which you can't control anyway), you will (paradoxically) achieve all you wish. We all acknowledge that perfection is unattainable, but that doesn't stop us from driving ourselves crazy in pursuit of it!

Let me suggest that it pays to change your attitude for one very simple reason: Your attitude is the *only* thing you *can* change! You can't control how others perceive you; you can't control their mood; you can't control what kind of day they are having; you can't even control why they are there in the room with you. So you may as well spend your energy working on yourself rather than on their thoughts. And if you decide that you are going to enjoy yourself, that your own enjoyment is the most important order of the day, you have a pretty good chance of it being contagious.

It helps to understand how emotions affect us. Why is joy powerful enough to cancel out fear? Because, as was pointed out earlier, a positive emotion and a negative emotion cannot coexist simultaneously. So if you make feeling good your mission, fear will dissipate on its own. You won't have to battle to overcome it.

As a public speaking coach, you might expect that I've had to deal with fear all the time. Well, you may have a hard time believing this—I certainly do—but in all the years I've been doing this work, paralyzing fear has never come up! I've often wondered, "Am I lucky enough to have attracted only the best of clients?" Hardly! So what is going on here?

I believe that my lack of formal training in public speaking gave me a leg up. I didn't know what to do about overcoming fear, so I chose to ignore it and get on with the business at hand, that of crafting the best possible speech—one that would be fun to deliver and fun to hear. I did not deny the fear. I acknowledged it, for about two minutes. I just never enlarged it by making it the topic of importance. I see fear here not as something to be conquered but as something to be bypassed. Moreover, most corporate clients come to me with precious little time to spare, so we don't have the luxury of exploring their fears. We must get down to work for a deadline that is ominously near. (The looming deadline is what strikes fear in *my* heart!)

Now I can explain the method to my madness. I don't believe in tackling fear for one reason: The more you tackle something, the more attention you must give it; and the more attention you give it, the more it grows. *To tackle fear means to shackle yourself to it.* I choose, instead, to think of fear as a roadblock: one that is stopping you from moving forward. You could expend a good deal of energy trying to move it, lift it, dynamite it out of existence. Or you could simply bypass it. Acknowledge its presence and take a detour around it. I see my job as leading you through the detour.

It is, I believe, fruitless to fight our fears. In doing so, we are fighting with reason what was not put there by reason. (Sort of like eating broth with a fork; the wrong instrument can never do the right job.) And fear is very personal. What terrifies one is innocuous to another.

More good news: *Fear is an inside job. It is created only in our mind.* So it can be bypassed when our mind is not focusing on the fear but on other, enjoyable tasks. Keep your mind engaged with pleasure and the fear will not be activated. And if not activated, fear is like a sleeping tiger—potentially dangerous but harmless when dormant. Dormant fear is not what stops us in our tracks. Only activated fear is crippling. And if your mind is busy with pleasure, there will be no room for panic, for here too, as in every other aspect of life, we can't hold opposing thoughts simultaneously.

If you expend your energy creating a fun story, a meaningful exchange, you will be so eager to share it that fear will vanish on its own. But let's distinguish here between fear and nerves. Fear can be crippling; nerves can be channeled. You actually want a certain amount of nervousness: it will keep you alert, pumped and primed. You want your adrenaline running. But you want it to serve you, not derail you. You don't want to be so relaxed that you look indifferent.

Remember: Say yes to excitement; the fear will disappear on its own.

"Dreams, unlike eggs,
don't hatch from sitting on them."
—It's the Thought That Counts

What If...

S peaking—in public and in private—assumes connecting to someone. I believe that the overwhelming fear
most have of public speaking stems from the possibility that we
will find ourselves disconnected, and thus, embarrassed. Our
nerves will get the best of us; we'll forget what we want to say;
we'll be laughed at; or we'll look stupid. (And that is just the
short list!) I am sure you can add your own nightmares. But I'd
rather, instead, have you consider these alternatives to dwelling
on your worst fears:

- What if, instead, we connected with our expertise? What
  if we shared what we love and know best?
- What if we crafted the best talk we were capable of? What
  if we liked our story so much that we couldn't wait to tell
  it?
- What if we rehearsed so thoroughly that our confidence
  level buoyed us onstage?
- What if we were assured our audience would love our
  message...be stimulated...be touched...be engaged?

I believe that connecting is the key to success: connecting
first to ourselves (through silence); connecting next to our story
(by revealing our passion about it); and finally connecting to our

audience (by getting real and dropping all pretense). When we feel confident that we can keep the connection, we lose ourselves in the process and forget about our nerves, our fears, and our shortcomings. Only then do we shine with a spark unique unto ourselves. Only then do we reveal our truest part. Only then do we engage others on a level that won't be forgotten.

No coach can teach you all you need to know. That you must find within. The best a coach can give you is the awareness that your job is, above all, to connect and help you find your own special way of doing just that.

> *"If at first you don't succeed...*
> *so much for skydiving."*
> —*After Dinner Speeches*

What Next...

Seasoned vs. Spontaneous

Now that the "secrets" of public speaking are out of the bag, what comes next? Being aware is not the same as taking action. So what are the actions you should take if you wish to shine as a public speaker? My answer is that of the New York cabbie when asked by a pedestrian, "How do you get to Carnegie Hall?" "*Practice, practice, practice!*"

There are no shortcuts to a great talk. No fool-proof recipes. No seven easy steps. The task requires focus, time, and effort—often in short supply if you're living in this hectic age of deadlines, emails, and interruptions.

Without practice, you may surprise yourself on stage. And that is not where you want to find surprises. Confidence comes from being in charge and being prepared. People often say to me, "I like to keep it spontaneous. I don't want to sound canned." To which I reply, "Being spontaneous *comes* from being prepared." If you don't rehearse in advance, you will be rehearsing on your audience. That is not fair to them and can't do justice to you.

One of my favorite comments came from a client with whom I had a running debate on how much he needed to prepare. He voted for less; I, for more. After a heavy day of testimony as an expert witness, he returned to the office, slumped at his desk, and said to me, "I never knew how much effort goes into *sounding* spontaneous!" I knew I had won the debate. The point is to sound spontaneous—not necessarily to make it up as you go along.

Above all, spontaneity comes from being relaxed. An unprepared speaker is a tense speaker. And a tense speaker can't afford to be spontaneous. He is too busy trying to mask his lack of preparation. Furthermore, even if he succeeds at sounding casual and breezy, his words will lack weight. His audience may, indeed, enjoy his off-the-cuff remarks, but they are not likely to retain them. But keep in mind an important distinction here. A very seasoned speaker who has prepared at length and has had much exposure at the podium can afford a certain amount of spontaneity. The years of practice allow her that luxury. As with any exercise, the more you do it, the stronger your muscles become. So if you wish to flex your speaking muscles, we come back to the mantra, "Practice, practice, practice."

The real reason for rehearsing is not what you might expect. It is not to polish the speech; it is to polish the speaker. It is to ensure that your confidence is well founded—not empty posturing. It is to ensure that you are at home with your message, that you can "wing it" if things go wrong, that you can afford to enjoy the moment instead of worrying about what comes next, and having to read continuously from notes—the kiss of death to spontaneity.

Again, spontaneous does not mean unprepared. Spontaneous means being *so* prepared that if the lights go out, PowerPoint crashes, and notes get lost, your message will still come through…and you won't look as if you've just survived a car wreck!

Every one of these situations I have observed. Those clients who were truly prepared sailed through the mishaps with humor and grace. Those who weren't, paid the price.

*"There's no fool
like an old fool."*
—Folk saying

Growing Old, Growing Up

T he following story, circulating anonymously on the Internet, illustrates my point about seasoning and spontaneity.

The first day of school, our professor introduced himself and challenged us to get to know someone we didn't already know. I stood up to look around when a gentle hand touched my shoulder. I turned around to find a wrinkled, little old lady beaming up at me with a smile that lit up her entire being.

She said, "Hi, handsome. My name is Rose. I'm eighty-seven years old. Can I give you a hug?"

I laughed and enthusiastically responded, "Of course you may," and she gave me a giant squeeze.

"Why are you in college at such a young, innocent age?" I asked.

"I'm here to meet a rich husband, get married, have a couple of children, and then retire and travel."

"No, seriously," I asked. I was curious what may have motivated her to be taking on this challenge at her age.

"I always dreamed of having a college education, and now I'm getting one!"

After class, we walked to the student union building and shared a chocolate milkshake. We became instant friends. Every day for the next three months, we would leave class together and talk nonstop. I was always mesmerized listening to this "time machine" as she shared her wisdom and experience with me.

Over the course of the year, Rose became a campus icon, and she easily made friends wherever she went. She loved to dress up, and she reveled in the attention bestowed upon her from the other students. She was living it up.

At the end of the semester, we invited Rose to speak at our football banquet. I'll never forget what she taught us. She was introduced and stepped up to the podium. As she began to deliver her prepared speech, she dropped her notecards on the floor. Frustrated and a little embarrassed, she leaned into the microphone and simply said, "I'm sorry. I'm so jittery. I gave up beer for Lent, and this whiskey is killing me! I'll never get my speech back in order, so let me just tell you what I know."

As we laughed, she cleared her throat and began:

"We do not stop playing because we are old; we grow old because we stop playing. There are only four secrets to staying young, being happy, and achieving success:

1. *You have to laugh and find humor every day.*
2. *You have to have a dream. When you lose your dreams, you die. We have so many people walking around who are dead and don't even know it!*
3. *There's a huge difference between growing older and growing up. If you are nineteen years old and lie in bed for one full year, and don't do a productive thing, you will turn twenty. Anybody can grow older. That doesn't take any talent or ability. The idea is to grow up by always finding the opportunity in change.*
4. *Have no regrets. The elderly don't usually have regrets for what we did, but rather for things we did not do. The only people who fear death are those with regrets."*

She concluded her speech by courageously singing "The Rose." She challenged each of us to study the lyrics and live them out in our daily lives.

At the year's end, Rose finished the college degree she had begun all those years ago. One week after graduation, Rose died peacefully in her sleep. Over two thousand college students attended her funeral, in tribute to the wonderful woman who taught by example that it's never too late to be all you can possibly be.

■ ■ ■ ■ ■

For Rose, life itself was preparation for her talk. For you, I wish the same.

If you speak from your heart about something you have lived (and loved), your preparation will serve you well. Your notes will not be necessary, just as they were not necessary for Rose. Your presence will suffice. For you to connect to the hearts and minds of your audience, you must first connect to your own. No speechwriter can do this for you.

Unless and until you sit down and dig deep within yourself about what is integral to you, the speech you craft will not have your voice. And without your voice, it will not soar.

The notes you carry up to the podium are merely your security blanket. Being tied to them lets you *think* you are prepared; but *being tied to your inner voice is what really grounds you.*

"And your point is?"
—Every listener to a
long-winded speaker

The Devil Is in the Details

While I maintain that if you can speak to one, you can speak to one hundred, I do not mean to imply that public speaking and private conversation are identical. They are the same skill but with a different spin.

In private, you can fish around in your mind until you formulate your thoughts; in public, you must know in advance what you wish to say, preferably without the "ums" and "ya knows." In private, you can ramble; in public, you had better have a point and get to it before the audience dies! In private, you are having a dialogue; in public, it is often a monologue. In private, you can be off-the-cuff; in public, you should have a plan.

Looking deeper at how they differ: In public speaking, there is always an agenda. You are there for one main reason. It might be to inform…to defend…to persuade…or explain; it may be to motivate, entertain, or inspire. Sometimes you have multiple agendas. But here's what matters most: *You can have only one message in public speaking.*

Having one message is not the same as saying the same thing again and again. Having one message means keeping your focus on the reason for being at the front of the room. It means that every part of your story, every aside in your delivery, every intention behind every line will support your perspective and your

71

point. It means having a point of view that is clear, consistent, and *personal*. Most of all, you must *keep it simple*.

Creating a speech is easy. Keeping it simple is the hard part!

Your point is not only about your topic. Your point is also about *you*. Why were *you* chosen to deliver this message? What do you bring to it of yourself, of your experience? What makes the talk unique to you?

Let's look here at the three stages of knowledge to understand where you fit in:

Stage one: *data collection*. This is the research you do when trying to understand a topic. Basically, it's the gathering of information.

Stage two: *analysis*. Here you make sense of the data. In analyzing, you break things down to understand how they work.

Stage three: *synthesis*. Here you reconfigure the parts into a *new* whole. You bring your insight to bear and lend a new slant to the analysis. You bring something of who you are and how you think.

Synthesis is where we get most creative. It is also where most people stop. They think their job ends with analysis. And what separates the top dogs from the pups is how they make knowledge their own; how they help others see a new picture through their eyes. *With synthesis, we learn not only about the thought, we learn about the thinker.*

Who you are is the point of your being onstage and not in the audience. Revealing yourself—how you think, what you hold dear—is what makes you interesting. It's not your research, your facts…it's *you!* Of course, revealing oneself is what sends most speakers into a twit. But once they get past that, they learn that the greatest rewards come with openness, for then (and only then) does real connection take place.

I spend much time, especially with my over-educated clients, arguing that facts and figures may seem like the foundation to persuasion but that they are just homework.

Passion is what really persuades. Joy is what really reaches others. If you take no pleasure in being at the podium, I guarantee your audience will take no pleasure that you're there either.

I have seen "well-prepared" speakers with copious notes send their audience into a stupor. And I have seen "disorganized" speakers rev them up. Don't misunderstand. For me, content is king. And I spend most of my time on it. But content without passion is boring, and content without joy, forgettable.

You may be wondering, "If joy is more vital than content, why not spend less time on the content and more on discovering the joy?" The answer is simple. Joy must derive from the content. What you say and how you say it must be integrated. *If you deliver good news for your company with a scowl on your face, we will believe your face and not your words.* The eye always wins out over the ear. Your credibility will always be compromised if your face or your tone negates your words.

The 7 Percent Solution: Substance vs. Style

Studies have shown that audiences recall only about 7 percent of what you say.

Imagine! All that research, preparation, and thought, and only a small fraction of what you've said will be retained. But there's more. They get their information from the 93 percent that comes from your demeanor, your style, your confidence, your mannerisms, your stance—in other words, your *body language*.

When I first heard this, I crumbled. I wondered if I had been giving all my efforts to the wrong component. But when I came to my senses, I realized that body language does not live in isolation. It is intimately tied to what you are saying—or should be. And when you are at ease with your content, your demeanor will convey your ease. When you find delight in your story, your body will convey delight.

The nonverbal must derive from the verbal. Style without substance is phony. And every audience has a finely tuned meter that registers phonies. When you are inauthentic, they sense it, much like the Supreme Court's definition of pornography: They "may not be able to define it, but they know it when they see it."

When it comes to body language, a coach and a video are most useful. I often just sit back and show a client her video with the sound off. It forces her to focus on her body: how stiff and forbidding it is; how frenetic and nervous it is; how boring, how inauthentic, how joyless, how charming. Whatever shows up, the client gains insight.

I once had a client tell me that what he got from watching his tape was that he had to buy a tie clip. His tie kept separating over his sizeable paunch, and it was very distracting to him. (Of course, losing a few pounds could have been another lesson, but we take from the session what we wish!)

Another time, I was viewing a videotape of a company star who had appeared on the *News Hour* on PBS the night before. I was in a small conference room with the president and a few others. I have no idea what was being said on the screen. Why? Because the sole woman on the panel of three had a lock of hair separate from a very precise hairdo. And I spent the bulk of the program wondering if her hair would ever fall back into place! I thought this was a "girl thing" and that I was the only one bothered by this (admittedly) minor event. Wrong!

When she finally shook her head and the wayward lock returned home, the president breathed a sigh of relief: "Thank God her hair fell back into place. I couldn't concentrate at all on what they were talking about." It just served to confirm that the devil truly is in the details.

I tell these stories not to make us all self-conscious to a fault. I tell them because the TV screen magnifies details, as does being on a podium. Since appearance can work for or against us, it pays to give our appearance some thought.

After a client has watched the video with the sound off, I turn on the sound, and again, the facts are there for the naked eye, and ear: Is the cadence of speech monotonous? Too fast? Too slow? Is the speaker connecting to his words emotionally or just reciting them? Is the speaker engaged with the audience or just gazing above the crowd? Is she smiling? Stone-faced? Just going through the motions? Turning her back to the audience to point at a screen? Mumbling? Fidgeting?

It may seem that we're traipsing through a minefield in this exercise, but that's only so when the speaker is not at ease. When finally at ease, all these issues magically disappear. For when we are most authentic, we are at our best because we relax. I say at our best—not at perfect. If you can forget perfect and be authentic, they'll love you and you'll love yourself.

I say this not theoretically. I say this because I have observed it time and again in my clients and in myself. Whenever we worry more about impressing others than expressing what is in our heart, we don't connect from our core. When we connect intellectually but not emotionally, we are offering only a meager part of ourselves—the part that lacks staying power... the part that may educate but fails to move.

*"Practice doesn't make perfect
if you're doing it wrong."*
—It's the Thought That Counts

Writer's Block: Two Kinds

Writer's block: Who hasn't felt it, and who hasn't cursed it? Some think it is when the muses fail to appear. I think not. I think it is when the critic gets the upper hand and gets to do his job before the writer gets to do hers. The critic within and the writer may be codependent, but they cannot cohabitate. The writer must be left to do her work *first*—with no concern for how wonderful the finished product will be. Only when the page is full can the critic don his hat and sharpen his blue pencil.

If the critic is sitting on the writer's shoulder whispering in her ear, "That's stupid," or "That's not what you really mean to say," the writer cancels the thought, the page remains blank (sometimes for days), and writer's block sets in.

The same holds true for the speaker. If you're having trouble putting your thoughts together, it is likely that the critic has taken up residence on your shoulder. Banish him! You can always fix what you've written later. But you can't fix a blank page.

Most often, though, I have encountered the opposite problem: people with *too much* to say.

A favorite client (engaging storyteller, passionate about ideas and gifted at connecting) called me in late one afternoon with writer's block—or so he thought. I didn't for one minute agree with him. I could see that something was tying him up, but it was not writer's block, which leaves one with a blank page. His problem was a multitude of pages, all of which were saying nothing (at least nothing intelligible).

Economists are known for analyses that give you, "On the one hand…on the other hand," until they seem to be describing an octopus. His paper had about eleven hands, which his audience could not keep track of, nor could he! So we talked, and talked, and talked well into the night. I kept trying to chop off a few limbs, but he kept creating new ones. The point of the speech kept eluding me. After hours, I still could not get a grip on his message. It finally occurred to me that we were swimming in facts and figures, but I needed a life raft called perspective.

I couldn't even tell if he was describing something valuable or harmful. The numbers kept sloshing around in my head. The facts had no context. The story, no plot. Simply put, there was no focus. I kept begging him for a headline—something that would define a conclusion. He tried but always ended up qualifying it, turning the headline into a paragraph…recreating the octopus!

We kept at it until nearly midnight. I kept insisting on a headline; he kept giving me multiple limbs. His aides were sitting around waiting to get the speech out for a 9:00 A.M. deadline and told me the next day that we were debating so vehemently, they feared we would start throwing things. And it was actually when he did throw something (his pencil up in the air) that I knew the battle was over. Out of sheer exasperation, when I said, "You've *got* to take a stand on this! Tell me in one sentence what you really feel?" he spat out a one-line conclusion that lent perspective to the whole issue. It may have been neater if we could have arrived at that point earlier. But I've come to understand that it was the hours of debating that allowed him to gain perspective. What his aides could not see was how much fun we were having, for he was a man who learned by arguing all sides against the middle. And I knew that if I stuck to my guns, he would see it my way because his way was just not working. I also came to see that those at the top of their game need an "opponent" who is not afraid...who would not give up and would not give in.

When it was over, he wrote his speech in less than an hour, with a precise focus now that he had taken a stand, now that he had gained a perspective.

Notice that I say *a* perspective. Singular. You can't have several. Not if you are to be authoritative.

The great challenge for analysts and academics is that they, indeed, must do their analyses from many angles. And that is as it should be. But when *reporting* their findings, they have to adopt a single perspective. A conclusion carries more weight—and is best remembered—if it says just one thing. Qualifying it will only water it down.

■ ■ ■ ■ ■

There are times, however, when the other kind of writer's block sets in: a blank page due to a dearth of ideas, burn-out, or other triggers. In each case, I advise silence. Don't fight the blank page; embrace it. Give in to it. Take a break. Step back from the void. Your creativity will return if you replenish your resources. Get creative about other things. Take a break, and *enjoy* it. Drop the guilt. Go for pleasure! As the Law of Attraction explains, fretting begets fretting; tension produces more tension. If you can switch gears and become creative about something ...anything, then the creativity will return to your writing as well.

> *"We attract not what we want*
> *so much as who we are."*
> —Anonymous

Getting Real:
The Key to Communicating

The Law of Attraction operates at all times, in all places, and in all of life. What we receive is a result, always, of what we put forth. So it pays to examine what we put forth when speaking to or with others.

How you meet someone's eye, how you hold her gaze, says as much about you as what you say. How you listen to her questions, how you deal with her feelings, speaks volumes and can obliterate words that don't match your behavior.

The real test of how well you communicate comes in the question-and-answer session after the formalities are over. This is where speakers "get real." This is where the monologue turns into a dialogue. This is where wooden speakers suddenly come alive; where tense speakers finally relax.

When clients watch themselves on videotape, they see the shift. And they like what they see. Why not, then, make the entire talk sound like a give-and-take? Why not ask the questions your listeners would if they could? Why not structure the talk so it sounds like a conversation rather than a speech?

It seems like a small tweak, but it makes a huge difference. When my clients hold a conversation rather than give a speech, an enormous weight lifts. They begin to enjoy themselves. Why? Because they feel the connection, and they know their audience is with them.

If you think your goal as a speaker is to cover your material, think again. It is, again and again, about connecting to your listeners. For that is where the fun is...no matter what your topic. It's a bit like going on a date. You think you've wowed your companion, showing off, looking smart, appealing, clever, sexy...only to find that your companion was not turned on by your smarts, your sex appeal, your achievements because all evening *you were not looking her in the eye*! You were having a date with yourself! The other was left out of the equation.

*"When you think you don't have time
to enjoy something, think again."*
—It's the Thought That Counts

Serious Fun

The more serious of my clients—lawyers, experts, corporate chiefs—do not expect to give talks that are fun. They bristle at first if I even hint at the prospect. They think they must come across as serious—and to most that means dull. But when they sit in the audience, they feel otherwise. They know as a member of the audience how easy it is to daydream, to think about their work, to show up in body but not in spirit.

So when charged with speaking, why do they forget their audience and think only of their topic? Habit is the culprit. They are used to doing speeches in a certain way, and God knows, they've sat through a lot of poor examples.

If we see something often enough, by sheer repetition, we begin to think that is the way it is done. It doesn't matter if the example is wrong. If it's repeated often, it becomes the norm. So let me remind you of the saying:

> *"If you always do what you always did,
> You'll always get what you always got."*

If you wish to change the outcome, first change your behavior. It may seem obvious, but how many times have we repeated an argument, an action, and expected our opponent to suddenly see the light? To paraphrase Albert Einstein, the solution will never be found by the same consciousness that created the problem.

I see my job as convincing you that being heard is not the same as being remembered. *If you wish to be remembered, get real.* Real with yourself. Real with your audience. *It's your vulnerabilities that allow us entry into the real you.* Your perfection, your façade keeps us out. In a small corner of our heart, we are saying to ourselves, "Yeah, it's okay for her to say…she's got it all." But when you are secure enough to reveal your shadow as well as your strength, then we feel a rapport. I heard Deepak Chopra say that we all have a shadow *because* we live in the light. Only beings that live in total darkness don't caste a shadow. Instead of trying to hide our shadow, we should thank it for making us more interesting.

It may appear that speaking in public is a one-way street (with all communication moving in one direction). But it is more like a rotary: What goes round comes round. If you understand where your listeners live, they will understand where you are coming from. We know instinctively when someone "gets" us. It goes far beyond an intellectual understanding. We feel heard, and we relax. Our defenses fall away. Our hearts open.

Always keep in mind that *people may not always remember what you've said, but they'll always remember how you made them feel.*

III.
THE DETAILS

*"It's not only what you bring to the table,
but how you serve it."*
—*It's the Thought That Counts*

Tell Me a Story:
If You Don't, I Won't Listen

S tory sells. (Advertisers know this.) Story convinces. (Marketers use this.) Story moves. (Authors know this.) Story defines. (We all know this.) At times we define ourselves with stories we accept from our fears: "I'm not smart enough. I'm not good enough. I'll never be rich. I'll never meet the right mate. I'll never get the knack for public speaking."

Change your story and you change your life. Again, the Law of Attraction is on your side. It will attract the positive when that is what you seek. It will also attract the negative if that is what you focus on, even if it is *not* what you consciously seek.

To echo an earlier chapter, silence and story go hand in hand. Your story lives inside of you, and the best way to unearth it is to calm down. Finding a good story will only happen when your creative juices are flowing. It will not come under stress. It will not come under duress. Go within, and you will discover what you really mean to say.

I knew an art director at a Madison Avenue firm who used to test new designs by asking his staff two questions:

1. Do you like it?
2. Do you *really* like it?

Always, it was the second answer that revealed the truth. Sometimes they matched; most often they did not.

It is tempting, in public speaking, to show off—to tell all you know. Resist this temptation. A talk must have a clear storyline with a single focus. The story may be short, it may be long. But it can't wander down multiple paths simultaneously.

Story protects you from saying things at random that will be retained for under thirty seconds. The best speakers come with a story that is as easy to hear as it is to tell. If we revisit our question of when private conversation turns into public discourse, the answer is "when story is the best way to convey your point."

Stories are effective in private dialogue, but they are not mandatory. In public speaking, however, if you don't have a clear story, your message will evaporate before the lights are turned up. Why is this? *Because we learn and remember through visual imagery.* This means pictures, not words. Why is it that the much-quoted, "A picture is worth a thousand words," seldom occurs to those giving presentations? It doesn't mean that you always have to show pictures: it does mean that *with your words* you must draw images. The words will fade; but the images will remain.

When words create pictures in our mind, the message sticks. And when the message sticks, it is because we hang it on the story. The real test of a good story comes if we can reiterate it a week later, a month later, or more. Visuals stay in our memory bank much longer than abstractions do primarily because abstractions can't be seen.

Here is an example of turning abstractions into concrete images:

—An economics professor walks into class on the first day of Economics 101. In typical academic fashion, he starts with a question and definition: "What is the study of economics about?

It is about the efficient allocation of scarce resources for the maximum utility of the public good." And the students yawn! They no better understand the subject than they did before class.

—Consider the approach of another professor. She walks in and asks different questions: "Do you have an allowance? What does it have to cover? Is there anything left over at the end of the month? How do you stretch your dollar? If you consider your allowance to be a scarce resource, and you have to stretch it to cover essentials, you are beginning to think like an economist. Economics is about making choices. We just use bigger words to describe the process."

The second professor builds her point inductively, through story and dialogue. Her questions are visual, real to the students, insuring that they will retain the information without having to memorize it.

The minute you abandon generalities and get specific (thus, visual), your speech improves immeasurably. Every writing class confirms this. You also become quotable, as a bonus. I began to see among my corporate clients that those who tell stories and create visual scenarios are those whose words show up in print.

I knew a president who was a master of visual language. He once said to me when I was feeling frustrated at getting a certain staff member to show up for meetings, "Oh, don't let him upset you. Getting him anywhere on time is like pushing a wet noodle up a hill!" I burst out laughing and never forgot his words because the image stuck.

■ ■ ■ ■ ■

Once Upon a Time...

What makes a good story?

There are as many answers to this question as there are stories. Some stories entertain; some persuade; some teach; some reveal aspects of ourselves that we may have only half known. Some move us to understand the world a bit better. Some give us insight into others.

It matters not whether we are trying to reach an audience of ten or ten thousand. Stories set the context; bring characters to life; move the plot (and our point) forward. Some stories keep us guessing. Some illuminate. But without a compelling story, the audience is lost—so, too, the speaker. With a compelling story, the speaker is not reliant on notes and is looking at the audience. An occasional glance at a list of points is sufficient to keep her on track.

Most of all, telling a story assures connection. Stories make us think, make us feel, move us to act, stir up our awareness. Why else would all cultures spend so many leisure hours at the movies, reading books, and attending plays? Why else would small children in all countries say, "Tell me a story."

If you wish to bypass the fear of speaking in public, work on a story that you'd love to tell. Make it interesting first to yourself—for only then can it intrigue anyone else.

"Life creates order,
but order does not create life."
—Antoine de St. Exupery

The Theme vs. the Point

A necessity in all speeches is a theme. The theme is not necessarily the point of the story, although it may be. A theme is what ties the various parts of the story together. Without a theme, the facts fall flat; figures swim around in our minds, and the point gets lost in a flurry of words.

Martin Luther King, Jr.'s classic "I Have a Dream" speech is known by its theme alone. A theme bears repetition, like a leitmotif in a symphony. A paper does not require a theme; a speech does, unless it's very short. *The ear cannot retain structure without repetition.*

A theme may present itself as you are crafting your story, but it is preferable if you know it in advance. It will keep you focused. It will focus your listeners. It will make your words easy to follow. It will make you easy to quote.

If I am listening to a client and cannot find a theme, chances are the talk is foggy. It amazes me how people improve once they find their theme, for then they know exactly where they are going and why they're going there. A good speech is only as good as its story line. And the story line is only as good as its theme.

The point, on the other hand, is why you're saying what you're saying. You can make it over and over without boring your audience if your theme and your point are connected. For example, suppose my point is "a speech without authenticity will fall flat." My theme might be "getting real."

The two are intimately linked. They can be seen as the same message using different words. But getting real is bigger, broader, more inclusive, *and* more quotable. I am making my point through examples of my theme even when my story may veer away for a while.

The Perfect Analogy

A client was facing his first jury trial as an expert. The stakes were huge since it was an anti-trust case, and by law, damages awarded in such cases are trebled. He was a well-known MIT professor, so he was used to facing a room full of students. But this situation had him worried.

In anti-trust cases, the outcome rests on the shoulders of the economic expert. If his story is convincing, a jury will be able to understand complex issues and make the right choice. If not, a great deal can be lost. And this case, at the time, was the largest anti-trust case ever to be tried. Coverage was not limited to the business section of newspapers; it made front-page headlines. Needless to say, the pressure was mounting.

His specific concern was that he would have just a few minutes to explain to the jury the distinction between causation and correlation—statistical concepts on which the case rested. He told me that it took him weeks to get his graduate students to fully understand the distinction, and he didn't see how he could present it to a jury in a matter of minutes.

I told him first that he had to stop comparing the jury to his students. The different audience required a different approach.

His graduate students required a much deeper understanding of the concepts than did the jury. Second, I assured him that there was a sure-fire way to reach the jury, and that was through analogy. We needed to find not just a casual analogy; it had to be a perfect fit. Easier said than done!

It took him, me, and two lawyers the better part of seven hours to find the perfect analogy. (It was possibly the most expensive analogy in the history of mankind! But given the stakes, worth every dollar.) We sifted through many might-have-beens, but only when we all agreed that the analogy fit exactly *and* was intuitively easy to grasp did we end our search. Time well spent...for it turned out that the analogy swung the jury in our favor, and the case settled. (Afterwards, when the jury members were interviewed, they corroborated that the analogy was what made the difference.)

The setup for our teaching analogy was simple: We used a picture of an elegant man and woman sitting in a Rolls Royce, dressed to the nines, going out for a night on the town. The dialogue was also simple: The expert was asked by his lawyer why he was showing this picture. He answered: "The couple in this ad are obviously rich; but the other side would have you believe that they *became* rich from driving a Rolls! And we all know how backwards that is. You have to *be* rich in order to buy the car; you don't get rich from driving it." He was then able to elaborate on the difference between causation and correlation without having to go into excruciating technical detail.

■ ■ ■ ■ ■

One reason that analogies have such power is that they are visual. But the real reason analogies work is the way they short-cut the learning process. By referring to something already known, we can slip in something unknown without having to take hours to explain it. Intuition fills in for thought.

Metaphors work in much the same way: If I say to you, "Getting him to be consistent is like trying to nail a custard pie to the wall!" you may not know all the details of the issue, but you will get the point.

Story might take many forms. But keep it simple and keep a single focus.

The Ear vs. the Eye

Telling a story and reading from a paper are not equal. But many confuse the two.

This comes out of fear. The mere thought of getting up in front of a room without every word written out gives people hives! It is also the kiss of death. The listener has to work too hard to "hear" a paper. It was, after all, conceived for the eye and not the ear. I became aware of this distinction early on, when I was just out of graduate school.

I was attending an academic conference in my field of communications. (At the time, when you said "communications," people did not assume you were in high tech; rather, they knew it meant people-to-people interaction.) The professors, in typical academic style, each got up and delivered papers—meaning, they wrote a paper and then proceeded to read it aloud, word for word. A crashing bore, one and all! Why?

First, a paper is read with the eye; a speech is heard with the ear. The two have different needs. The ear needs shorter sentences, a different structure, thematic repetition, and a host of other tricks of the trade. *The eye can look back; the ear can't hear back.* The spoken word is gone with the wind. (And with the long-winded, it is gone even before the end of the sentence.)

Second, unless you happen to be Laurence Olivier or Meryl

Streep, you probably read aloud in a monotone. It happens to the best of us.

Reading aloud flattens intonation, the rise and fall of natural speech. When that happens, emphasis is lost, and everything begins to sound the same. And the audience wants to nap. The natural cadence of a speaker, hesitant and imperfect though it may be, becomes homogenized and lacks the quirks that make us unique.

At this particular conference, however, they chose a keynote speaker who saved the day. He was a marvel to us all. He spoke without notes. He spoke with passion, authority, and humor. He made each of us feel that he was speaking to us alone, in a normal tone of voice, having an intimate chat. His own comfort level made each of us feel at home. His topic reached us where we lived. It was not academic. It was personal.

More than thirty years have passed since I sat in that audience, listening to Dr. Neil Postman of New York University discuss his book, *Crazy Talk, Stupid Talk*. And to this day, he remains for me the gold standard of what a great speaker can do. He made us think; he made us laugh; he challenged our assumptions. Above all, he proved to me that having a conversation is no different whether you are talking to one or to five hundred in the room. Today, I remember not a word of the other speakers (or paper deliverers).

But Neil Postman's example is foremost in my mind, for he gave me this insight:

> *When we are comfortable within ourselves,*
> *we allow others to join us there; and when we*
> *are all comfortable together, real connection occurs.*
> *Numbers don't matter. Connecting does.*

■ ■ ■ ■ ■

Recently, I was privileged to hear Jane Goodall, Ph.D., the primatologist who forever changed our understanding of chimpanzees and their social structure. She, too, was a keynote speaker at a conference sponsored by the Omega Institute. She, too, spoke without notes. She, too, made us laugh, made us feel. She, too, was so comfortable within herself that we were put at ease by her mere presence. She used no slides, no tricks, no gimmicks to get our attention. Dr. Goodall exuded the confidence that came from a life well-lived; she exuded humility as a servant of the planet and the animals she so adores. The audience of two thousand was riveted. Not a sound was made for forty-five minutes.

This is a high standard, indeed. But what I take away from examples such as these is that *the best of the best speak simply and from the heart.* They don't need word slides. They tell a personal story and make it relevant to their audience. They are not self-conscious…just very, very aware.

"Pure logic is the ruin of the spirit."
—Antoine de Saint Exupery

*"There are all kinds of truths. There is the truth of
illness and the truth of wellness. Choose the truth that
serves you. What you are living is your truth."*
—Abraham-Hicks

Eye Contact: It's Not a Spectator Sport

The capital crime committed by many speakers comes
from the very act of reading—they must *look down* at
their notes. Thus, they fail to make eye contact. This means that
connection is occurring between them and their notes, not between them and their audience. So I am here again to state the
obvious: *If you don't look at your audience, they won't be looking at you.*
And if they don't look at you, they are losing the 93 percent of
what you communicate through body language. So, if you don't
look at them, and they're not looking at you, the question becomes, "Why are you speaking to them in the first place?"

Eye contact is not window dressing. It is the vital link between
the listener and the speaker. It is not about style; it is about truth. We
all know from life that someone who can't look you straight in the
eye is someone you are not likely to trust. Why should it, then, be
different just because you are at a podium?

Reading from notes may make you feel secure, but *you would
be far better off if, at the expense of sounding perfect, you sounded real.* An
audience may admire a glib speaker, but they relate more to a
sincere one.

Most of my clients come wanting to sound like some ideal
they have conjured up. They leave, instead, sounding like them-

selves—which is all I could hope for. That is the basis of real security: not notes, not visual aids. Finding your own voice is what puts you at ease and allows you to put others at ease. Finding your own voice is, above all, what no one can take away from you. It is the refuge of the timid; the solace of the frightened; the bedrock of the orator.

The recurring lesson I have learned over the years is this: If your voice is not authentic, you will always experience a disconnect. And *fear arises only when we are disconnected from our true selves.* As Shakespeare says in Hamlet: "This above all, to thine own self be true, and it follows as the night the day, thou cans't not then be false to any man."

When you do connect, you will enjoy the act of public speaking. I promise you that.

I've seen it happen again and again. It cannot be otherwise. It happens for the skilled speaker and for the novice alike.

A dear friend, age ninety-one, is a bit of a celebrity at the place where she does volunteer work. Her eyesight is failing now but she still goes into the office three mornings a week to help out. She read a first draft of my book and to her surprise (and to my amazement) had her first public speaking engagement a few weeks later. She was asked to speak before a large audience at a community center about her work and her career. She had prepared a script, rehearsed it several times, but realized onstage that she could not easily read in the dim light. So she figured that connecting was the name of the game and simply looked out at the audience and told them her story.

Silence, story, awareness. Your best allies. Leave your notes behind. Your allies will keep you company.

> *"Before you speak, ask yourself:*
> *Is it kind, is it necessary, is it true?*
> *Does it improve on the silence?"*
> —Shirdi Sai Baba

Our Spirit vs. Our Brain

I came upon the quote above while on a yoga retreat at Kripalu in the Berkshires. It was posted on the door of an office, admonishing those about to knock to consider their words. I have no doubt that the world would be a much finer place if we all took this saying to heart. So often, I find that people only consider whether something is true—as if truth alone gives us license to speak our mind. But if we ask ourselves, "Is what I am about to say kind? Is it necessary?" we may find that truth alone does not serve us.

If our words damage a relationship, if they serve no higher purpose than to prove us "right," what do we gain from uttering them? And what do our listeners gain from hearing them? If we spent a few seconds screening our words before we utter them, we would save ourselves the trouble of later on having to eat them!

People process language not only with their ears but with their spirit. And spirit responds to positive thoughts. It also has a much longer memory.

Our spirit is always awake. Our brain is often asleep. When we feel overloaded, our brain shuts down. In our oversaturated media culture, we are constantly bombarded with information.

We can't retain most of it, nor would we want to. But our spirit can always tell when something is important. Short-term memory is where we store the trivia we don't need for long. Long-term memory is where we store messages that have meaning for us. I've noticed that most technical speakers inadvertently aim for the short-term, that is, they rely on facts and figures, which simply don't stick for long. Stories, however, do last, partly because they make us feel. And *feelings are the language of spirit.*

This distinction is useful when vying for the attention of your audience. They have husbands, wives, lovers (not necessarily at the same time); children, bosses, chores; worries about what to have for dinner, about that memo that must get out, and about whether our nation is going to hell in a hand basket while all of this is going on. *If you wish to be remembered, you must engage more than their brains.* They may not be able to quote your exact words, but they will carry with them your intentions.

So how do you ensure a captive audience? Again, we come back to story. To create a compelling story, first *you* must like telling it. (Sounds like common sense. But common sense is often called the least common of all the senses!) Second, your audience has to like it, which presumes knowing who your audience is—not in general, not vaguely, but as specifically as possible.

You wouldn't explain a concept the same way to a seven-year-old as to a seventeen-year-old. Knowing your audience takes research. The more you know, the more you'll be able to connect.

Think about your listeners:

- Have they been sitting in that conference hall for two days by the time you speak to them?
- Have they been bored? Engaged? Active in the Q&A?
- Are they thinking about lunch? The plane they have to make in three hours?
- Are they decision-makers? Technocrats? A mix?

- Do they regard your topic as a nuisance? A godsend? A bore?
- Are you a stranger to them? A colleague? Feared? Revered? Neutral?
- Do you even know? If not, find out!

I once watched a very good speaker fail miserably. He had assumed the presidency of his firm not long before and was reporting on the massive reorganization he had undertaken with the help of an army of consultants. The new plan had been "hush-hush" to all but a few directors, and the secrecy surrounding it worried his senior staff. They were concerned about how the restructuring would affect their pay, their workload, and their title. They were worried but curious: some dubious, some neutral. They came from around the world for the unveiling of the plan at a two-day conference.

If the president (by his own admission not a "people person") had had his finger on the pulse of the group, he could have put their fears to rest. Instead, he went through painstaking detail about the reorganization without ever addressing their emotional needs. He sounded less like a leader and every bit like a technocrat going over the minutia of the plan, complete with boring slides.

They wanted reassurance; he gave them facts. They wanted passion; he gave them trivia. They wanted vision; he gave them numbers.

As we broke for lunch, a senior VP escorted me to the dining room. He *was* a people-person and privy to the details of the plan. So when he asked me what I thought of its unveiling, I told him the truth. He took it in. And before the day was over, he got up and gave an empassioned, impromptu talk about the excitement he felt as they were entering this new era for the firm. He hit every empowering thought on how they would be better off, freer to work in a decentralized organization, how they could take charge of their own sectors and reap the rewards that were now built in for them. He did not linger on minutia. He spoke from genuine excitement, and his passion saved the day.

Were it not for this man, the group would have left as confused as before and twice as hostile. Thanks to him, they shared a newfound optimism—all because he bothered to view the world from their shoes.

■ ■ ■ ■ ■

At another conference, an economist told me that she was sitting next to a commissioner for the electric utility industry. This man was gifted at making origami figures—his pastime when he was especially bored. Before the end of the two days, he had a veritable menagerie of animals lined up before him on the table.

So watch for signs of boredom. Switch gears if you have to. Make sure your preparation allows for wiggle room if you have to change the pace, change the subject or wake up a dozing group.

Follow the tactics of another client who was trying to carry out an assignment he had been given the night before. It was to explain a technical problem to a group with no technical expertise in his subject. He knew when he was losing the group as he saw them getting glassy-eyed. So he stopped short and said, "I can see that I'm losing you. Let me try this another way." When, a few minutes later, they once again were lost, he stopped again, and said: "This time, I've not only lost you, I've lost myself! In fact, when I tried this on my wife at breakfast, I lost her too. So I'm going to try once more, and if I fail, I'll just sit down." (Now that, in my book, is confidence!)

The audience loved his candor and listened with great attention, really pulling for him. And the third time was the charm—partly because he had worked out the kinks and partly because they were rooting for him to succeed.

Bear in mind, that your audience *wants* you to succeed. Even if they are critical before you open your mouth, they would rather be enthralled than bored. No one wants to feel that he is wasting his time. If they want to debate with you in the Q&A, take it as a sign of engagement. An angry audience is preferable to an apathetic one. Anger you can work with; apathy leaves you little recourse.

■ ■ ■ ■

From coaching and observing people in the top ranks of corporate America, I am struck by how leaders are not afraid to show their humanity. They want to share the fire in their belly. And though they may hire others to push paper, they are never above paying attention to detail. I once had an executive ask me to please make sure his staff did not turn their pages at the podium but slid them aside, thus not bringing attention to their notes. (I assured him that if I had my way, they wouldn't be carrying a stack of notes up to the podium in the first place.)

The best leaders don't lead by bullying people or imposing their will. They share their vision. And sharing implies listening, not just telling. Listening well and communicating often are the allies of leaders. No matter what their style, these traits prevail.

I must admit that before I had close contact with corporate leaders, I assumed that many rose to the top by stepping over dead bodies. I was dead wrong! The CEOs I have known have been role models for me. I once asked the head of a global company where he acquired his "people" skills. His words were telling: "At my kitchen table…listening to my wife and daughters work out their differences and share their feelings." (How could I not love the guy?)

Many books these days are written about leadership and about the need for emotional intelligence (EQ). So far, our culture has fostered intelligence only from the neck up. And we are seeing the skewed results of that approach. Until we foster intelligence that integrates all of who we are, we are showing up at the podium fragmented and incomplete. I sincerely believe this is why we are reluctant to embrace public speaking. One thing I know for sure:

When you are on a podium, a dais, or a TV screen, everything *about you is magnified; the visible as well as the invisible qualities that make up who you are. So become aware of who you are—in body, mind, and spirit.* For any separation within yourself will serve only to separate you from your listeners.

> *"There's no such thing as good writing;*
> *there's only good re-writing."*
> —Louis D. Brandeis

Too Busy for Words

Many a CEO, director, and senior VP think it impossible to carve out time to rehearse an important speech. They think their time is best spent editing—for the fifth time—a speech drafted by their writers. I try to convince them that the *only* task of value is finding the words within themselves.

Being tied to notes is like being tied to a security blanket. It's time to give it up! (You can bring the blanket with you, but you don't want to depend on it.)

I will admit that in our hectic lives, time is hard to come by. That's why I have found myself holding sessions in airplanes and in limousines to the airport on evenings when I should have been at my own dinner party. These unlikely moments aren't necessarily the norm, but I've felt that if a person is willing to make the time, I will find the way to be there.

But what if you really don't have time to work with a coach— or even a staff member? Well, there's always your mirror, your cat, or your seventeen-year-old daughter (who'd probably rather be out with friends).

A name partner in a law firm, whose writing I admired, told me that he would routinely run his important briefs by his sixteen-year-old daughter. Whatever she couldn't follow, he knew needed work. "But then," he told me, "she went off to college and took up sociology…and was of no use to me any longer." The volume of jargon she acquired ruined her keen ear for simple language and direct talk—elements that are vital before a jury.

If you can corral anyone—animate or inanimate—do speak your words *out loud*. Reciting them to yourself is not enough. You must hear what you are about to say, just as your audience will be hearing and not reading.

I once was reading a passage to a friend on the phone, asking her to choose the best of two versions. (When I write, I read my work out loud to test how conversational it is. If it's listenable, it will be readable.) I noticed as I was reading to my friend that each time I said something that resonated for her, she unconsciously said "hmm." Although I was not actively counting the "hmms," I was aware that one version had elicited far more notes of approval than the other. I teased her about the "hmm factor," as I started calling it, as good an indication as any to tell if you are hitting the mark.

I suggest that when you are facing a deadline with little time for editing, find someone who will read your own work out loud *to you*. Just listen. Don't read along. Don't interrupt. *Your ear will pick up what your eye will miss.* If the reader stumbles often or can't get the rhythm of the piece, chances are it is awkward and lumbering. If it flows and is music to the ear, it will work for the eye.

My friend's "hmms" came when I was saying things that were thought-provoking, that she was seeing in a new light. After a while, I noted that each one corresponded to a thought that had excited me as well as I was writing it. That's how I knew my work was done. The connection had been made.

You can never be sure what will resonate with your audience. You can only know what resonates for yourself. And if you write true—true to yourself—you will attract an audience that wants to listen.

Another thing I know for sure:

Most of us expend vast amounts of energy putting up a good façade—trying to appear confident when we are not; trying to look in charge when we don't know what the hell is going on; trying to hide our vulnerabilities when we fear they will indicate just how soft our hearts are. This is as true when we are among friends as it is when we are at the podium.

But when I probe a bit and ask people to recall a moment when they *did* dare to share their vulnerabilities—when they did open up without filtering their feelings, they admit that they were not weakened by the revelation—they were, in fact, strengthened by it. Call it human kindness. Call it grace.

Time and again, I find that when we get real with one another, that's when genuine connection (and inspiration) shows up. It does not show up as a result of media training; nor the outcome of focus groups; it is not the stuff of political polls. When we find the courage to reveal our personal truths, we allow others to do the same. If nothing else, they will connect to us because *most often a personal truth is also a universal one.*

It is because of this universality that books, plays, films—all of which are specific to the character, plot, locale of the story—have such mass appeal. A tale of someone you've never met, in a place you've never known, in a time you've never lived, in a situation you've never imagined can resonate as if it were an intimate experience.

Such is the power of revelation; such is the power of truth.

Remember when you face an audience, whether in the voice of a playwright or as a public speaker, *your vulnerabilities and your quirks make up the whole of who you are;* they also serve to distinguish you from others. Trying to suppress them leads only to an unauthentic you. And when you show up inauthentically, you can't relax and you can't shine. Your truth, warts and all, is more intriguing than a façade ever could be.

"When you compete with yourself,
you both win."
—*It's the Thought That Counts*

Hidden Dimensions

When I was a child in the 1950s, certain movies were filmed in 3D, requiring paper glasses with special lenses that were handed out with your ticket. They allowed you to see in three dimensions, adding depth to the screen and fullness to the characters. The films were not noteworthy, the glasses cumbersome—and the fad passed.

I think of it at times after I've interviewed a new client. They come in, we chat, we share, we laugh. I find them charming, intelligent, genuine. It is always my favorite part of the day. Then, they leave, and I read what they've written or I watch them on video giving a talk. What a difference! I'm usually left wondering, "Who is this tight, dull person? What happened to their personality?"

Many believe, erroneously, that in the workplace, we must park our personalities with our car...to be picked up when we leave the office. I don't know where this idea originated, but it serves no one.

No one voluntarily chooses to become two-dimensional—flat, diminished, and colorless. But in the name of looking professional, this transformation occurs unwittingly. So monitor yourself. Make sure you feel authentic every time you speak. Like any habit, when practiced, it becomes natural. And only when it becomes natural to be yourself can you step up to a podium and show up as the real you—without worry, without fear...rather, with pride and charm.

*"Don't worry that you'll take a shot and you'll miss.
The fact is you'll miss every shot you don't take."*

—Anonymous

Famous Last Words

W hat are you going to do this weekend while you're watching the kids?" my friend Esther Shaw asked her husband on the way out to work. Out of left field came his answer: "I think I'll write a comedy about your catering business." (Esther owned a kosher catering company staffed entirely by Italian waiters—surely the stuff of incipient humor.) But in all his forty-five years, Arje, her husband, had never written a play...not even a sketch...not a story, nothing!

"Okay, if that's what you want to do...but you're not funny and you can't write. Have a good time!" and off she went. (Esther was generally regarded as the funny one in the household, so her remark was said in good humor.)

"You're not funny and you can't write" are words that Esther ended up eating. For Arje not only crafted *A Catered Affair* (which, of course, took far longer than a weekend), but his next play, *The Gathering*, made it to Broadway and another play, *Magic Hands Freddy*, played off Broadway—both with reviews that belie the fact that he had not started writing until middle age.

I had never heard of Arje Shaw until I attended a staged reading of *The Gathering*, a play that shook me to my core. Nor had anyone else heard of him, for his was a journey from obscurity to Broadway, the stuff most others only dream about. Although his play was not the first that moved me deeply, it was the first that moved me to part with some money. I became Arje's first investor, something that surprised him (money coming in from a total stranger) and shocked me (I had never done *anything* like that before and did it at a time when my business was in a lull).

But I didn't even stop to think. I knew this was something I had to do. So Arje and I took risks together. "If you are looking for a surefire way to lose money, put it into an unknown play by an unproven playwright," my brain was telling me. But my heart said that the healing message in this funny play about a serious subject had to be seen. And I didn't care if I realized no returns; I wasn't in it for the money.

Not only did I get my money back, I made lifelong friends in Arje and Esther Shaw. Together we took a wild ride. The obstacles seemed never-ending—from the difficulty of raising capital for a New York production when no one knows your name, to the contracts with theatres that are free one moment and booked the next; from dealing with unions, actors, egos, fears, emotions, air conditioners that fail in 97-degree heat, down to publicity that doesn't get out on time.

The obstacles kept coming. The point is that there will always be obstacles. It's called Life! *How we choose to face those obstacles determines whether we will blossom or remain tight in the bud.*

I also experienced first-hand Arje's belief in his work and how the Law of Attraction will bend the world to your dreams. Arje Shaw exemplifies how living your dreams means taking calculated risks. As Bob Proctor, the success coach, says, "You can't steal second base with your foot on first."

Progress involves risk. And if we are to live our best lives— not just the safest ones—we must risk what we believe in. So I urge you: Go to the podium prepared to take risks. Risk being open. Risk sharing your heart. And the world will bend to *your* dreams.

> *"Love is not thinking, but being."*
> —Antoine de St. Exupery

Yoga and Public Speaking

I have practiced yoga long before there was a yoga studio on every third block of New York and almost every town in America. At first, in the late sixties, I did yoga simply because it felt so good. I was not a serious student of the discipline. I had no interest in meditation, and I couldn't have cared less about Sanskrit or the history of the practice. I simply wanted to reap the physical benefits of flexibility and the psychological benefits of inner peace.

Then the magic took over. I felt calmer, surer, clearer in my life. There was no space for falseness, pettiness, or anger over minor infractions. I found myself making choices and decisions from a place of knowing, not thinking. My instincts seemed heightened. My outlook more serene.

These were subtle effects. No major revelations. No Kundalini experiences shooting wild energy up my spine. No trumpets blaring to announce a new me.

But I did begin to notice that my work with clients was being subtly affected. I listened differently. I had always listened well. But *I used to listen to words. Now I was listening for voice.* Because yoga united me with my own voice, with my own truth, I was more able to detect these qualities in others.

I became a tuning fork for authenticity. If something did not resonate within me as honest, I knew there was work to be done. Oddly, my intuition proved right—always.

Sometimes, people don't even know when they are lying to themselves. And it might take a simple question for them to realize that what they said, they don't quite believe.

Yoga means to unite, to bind together. It fosters the uniting of body, mind, and spirit. Public speaking also is an act that is meant to unite—uniting you with your listeners. When you unite first to your spirit, then to your audience, you become aware that the message that leaves your heart reaches theirs. Then all fear falls away. Then you are at home in front of a room. There you find connection. There you find joy.

In my practice of yoga and its subtle influence on my work none of these insights were even conscious when they first started. I just became aware of a certain magic when I was with people. I was able to sit quietly and really be with them. Not from a place of judgment...nor from a place of manipulation. I didn't want anything from them except connection. And I found that I could connect best when they were connected to themselves.

For years, I was reluctant to analyze what was happening for fear that shining a light on the magic would cause it to disappear. But as I expanded my own understanding, I came to see that it was not magic at all. It was, rather, a process that everyone is capable of and that, if we choose, we all engage in: connecting to our own truth.

What does this actually look like? What was I sensing or seeing in my clients when they were connecting to themselves?

With some, their eyes sparkled as if lit from within. With others, their body language changed: Some became more relaxed; some, more animated. Still others moved from being matter-of-fact to being engaged; some, from sounding businesslike to sounding sincere. And still others moved from being dull to being passionate. With some, the change meant being funny instead of factual; light-hearted instead of heavy.

The transformation took different forms. But the common denominator could not be missed. After the magic set in, they loosened up; they got in touch with something genuine. They achieved authority without having to chase it. Or fake it. And above all, they started having a good time.

Fun is only possible when you are relaxed enough to let it happen. And letting it happen is at the heart of connection. You can't force connection any more than you can force spirit. And you can't force fun any more than you can force connection. *You cannot muscle your way into fun. You must surrender to it.*

Surrendering to anything is, perhaps, one of the hardest feats in our culture.

We are trained to work hard, to effort our way into what we are seeking. Type A personalities are admired. Relaxing, releasing our goals, enjoying the moment for what it offers are not part of our mindset. And that is why we have to get out of our minds! Emotional intelligence *must* become as respected as mental acuity. We must cultivate instinct, intuition, and impulse if we are to live fuller lives.

What I am suggesting here may be radical to some and obvious to others:

If we want the podium to feel like home, we must first be at home within ourselves.

Future Goals, Present Action

When we are on stage, whether as a speaker, an actor, or an expert witness, we may show up with goals, but *if we focus on the goal and not on the moment, we are likely to lose the connection.* Why is this so? Because our talk is happening in the Now. Goals take place in the future, and we can't legislate the future. We have access only to what's happening right now. So our power to control is always in the present. Consider this parable:

A young but earnest Zen student approached his teacher and asked the Zen master: "If I work very hard and diligently, how long will it take for me to find Zen?"

The master thought about this, then replied, "Ten years."

The student then said, "But what if I work very, very hard and really apply myself to learn fast. How long then?"

Replied the master, "Well, twenty years."

"But, if I really, really work at it. How long then?" asked the student.

"Thirty years," replied the master.

"But I do not understand," said the disappointed student. "At each time that I say I will work harder, you say it will take me longer. Why do you say that?"

Replied the master, "When you have one eye on the goal, you only have one eye on the path."

Your goal may be to sound authoritative, and that is fine to think about in planning your remarks. But when on stage, forget authoritative—think about connecting. I have worked with some of the most seasoned and skilled speakers in their fields. They work hard on the content, but when the time comes to deliver, their sole focus is on reading their audience—not their notes.

Our goals will take care of themselves when we let them go—not by denying them, but by focusing on what makes us feel good. This is explained by another teaching from Abraham. They explain that we set up our future by what we *think* in the present coupled with how we *feel*. Feelings give power to our thoughts. They refer to this as pre-paving. You are creating your future road by feeling good, relaxing, releasing resistance to what life hands you, and enjoying the moment. It is not necessary (contrary to many other teachings) to pursue your goals with sweat and pain; by allowing them to unfold naturally, you will get what you need *and* enjoy the ride.

In the Beginning...

We all would like to imagine that we are writing for a reader who is relaxed and interested, sitting in a comfortable arm chair, feet propped up, the dog snuggled by his side, and ready to give the text his undivided attention. Dream on!

In today's world our writing is meant to attract busy, often harried readers: those with phones ringing, people interrupting, fires to be put out, and so much on their minds that the word concentration for them refers only to frozen orange juice!

The same holds for speakers. We would like to think that a room full of bodies is a room full of minds. But we know better from our own behavior; while the bodies show up, the minds can be anywhere but there.

The bad news is that the speaker has approximately thirty seconds to grab the audience's attention before they shut down. During that time, if she doesn't say something engaging, intriguing or amusing, she may never get them back. The good news is that if you realize this, you can do something about it. You can present a compelling fact that will surprise your listeners; you can tell a personal anecdote that will engage them; you can make them laugh, not with a warm-up joke, but by sharing humor relevant to your tale.

In looking at how to begin a talk, it's important to look at how *not* to begin. Don't begin with housekeeping announcements, boring acknowledgments, or trivia. Save that for the end, if you must. Say something of interest. And make sure you aim at the level of your audience. You wouldn't explain statistics the same way to your grandmother as you would to a room-full of Ph.D. candidates. (I once said this to a young man who then told me his grandmother was among the very first Ph.D.s in his native country. So much for generalizations!)

If you are speaking on a technical subject to a lay audience, you have even more to consider. Make sure you start at the beginning—*not* for you but for *them*. What you consider to be the beginning is likely to assume too much. Make sure you go back to square one for your audience. (This is where a coach can be a big help. Her eyes will glaze over until you get it right.)

You will have to set the context before you can launch into your narrative. You will have to specify why your story is meaningful, why the audience should care.

What follows is a simple example (paraphrased) from Nora Ephron—journalist, screenwriter, director—giving a talk on her career.

While Nora was studying to be a journalist, her professor gave the following list of facts (known as the five Ws) that were to be included in an article:

Who:	schools in Sacramento
When:	next Thursday
What:	will receive specialized training
Where:	in L.A.
Why:	for continuing education

They went to their typewriters and each produced a lead sentence incorporating the five Ws, each version merely rearranging the facts they had been given. The professor read them, and one by one, threw each into the trash basket. He looked at the group, shaking his head, and told them that the only way to write this lead is: "Schools will be closed next Thursday." We all laughed, recalling how many times we recited information when we needed, instead, to interpret it.

I *loved* this example because I read or hear information so often that I understand...I just don't know *why* I'm getting it. I am forever saying to my clients: "What does this *mean?*" Your audience needs results. They want conclusions, not simply data.

■ ■ ■ ■ ■

When I first started my career, like most mortals, I was embarrassed to parade my ignorance before my clients. Then I saw that they were always grateful. When I didn't understand, it meant that others wouldn't understand either. They learned that when they are too close to a subject, they assume too much about it. They need to go back to square one. The problem, though, is when you are comfortable in your knowledge, you may have forgotten where square one is!

Here is a story from a favorite client—a seasoned economist, a great teacher, and a man comfortable in his own skin.

He was to appear before a jury in San Francisco. For days, his staff had prepared a large visual aid to help the jury understand the statistics of the case. It showed a bar chart with horizontal bars in descending order—the largest bar at the top, smallest at the bottom. About midway through his explanation, he had a funny feeling that the jury was misinterpreting the chart. They saw the top bar as a *good* thing. It was, after all, the biggest bar, and most often we equate big with best.

The economist, however, was trying to illustrate it as a bad thing for his clients. And because he was tuned in to the jury, he reversed course and said: "Let me be clear: Think of these bars as representing illness. The top bar shows how much cancer you have. You would not consider this good news. You want to be at the bottom of the chart, not at the top."

Note that the chart was seemingly clear to all the economists who put it together for the trial. But not for the jury! The meaning for them was not self-evident until it was properly interpreted.

So I caution you: Do not assume anything. Make sure you are looking at complex information through the eyes of the uninitiated. You don't want to "talk down" to your audience. You also don't want to leave them in the dust as you forge ahead through assumptions that you never took the time to spell out.

Egg on Your Face

Back to how to begin a talk—or not.

There is no single best way. But there is a way that is so tired and trite that it is best avoided: the opening joke.

Admittedly, the opening joke, originally meant to warm up the audience (and the speaker), meant to establish rapport and show how human we all are that we can laugh together, aimed for high ideals. But consider this: Not everyone has the timing or ease of a Bob Hope (who used silence to great effect, as do most comedians). So two things can result:

1. The joke bombs; you stand there with egg on your face, feeling embarrassed and inept.

2. The joke succeeds; you are looking good; the audience is primed. Then what happens? You get serious! You become dryer by the minute; all the good will and connection fade away, leaving your audience feeling manipulated and asking themselves, "Where did the funny guy go?"

Don't get me wrong. I encourage humor and enjoy nothing more than a serious point cloaked in humor. But more often than not, the opening joke is not intimately related to the topic, and the audience feels manipulated because they have heard it used too often as a device. They are smart enough to recognize it for what it is—nothing more than an ice-breaker, not relevant to the speech.

It is far wiser to weave humor *throughout* the talk. Or to use it when least expected and catch your listeners by surprise. My wish for you is that you achieve the goals of the opening joke *throughout* the talk, not merely in the first two minutes.

When all is said and done, how should you start?

Decide first what your goal is. Is it to entertain? To inspire? To educate? To challenge? Is it all of the above?

Then ask yourself how well you know your audience, as I've discussed earlier.

Your opening must fit your goal. Here are a few examples:

- Use a personal anecdote (not a joke, but a short tale). Help them picture a scene.
- Create a little movie playing in their minds. Get them involved in the action or the outcome. Surprise them! Everyone loves a good story, and if you can lace it with humor, all the better. But your story must be relevant to your audience's interests.
- Do take the time to find out about them. It will pay off handsomely.

Here is the opening of a talk that a male economist used when speaking to a group of professional women in economics. He was their keynote speaker, and a highly-regarded consultant as well as a charming raconteur. He started out (loosely paraphrased):

"I am in good company here today. As I was preparing my talk, I came to realize that the two prevalent schools of thought in economic forecasting are both based on the outlook of a well-known woman: the first is that of Shirley Temple in the Good

Ship Lollipop—who saw only sunny skies and happy landings in the future; the second is that of the Greek Cassandra, who saw the sky falling all around, all the time."

He developed these two themes, always lightheartedly, referring to the power of women to influence how the world sees itself. It was fun to listen to, informative, chatty, and targeted for his audience.

Another client, an investment banker, was about to discuss the issue of health care in America. She was on a panel and wanted to say something that would make her stand out from the others. Since she was comfortable with speaking directly to people in small groups, we decided that she should flip the usual format on its head and *start* with a Q&A session.

"How many of you have been hospitalized within the past year, or have had a family member in the hospital?" (A few hands went up.)

"Tell me about your experience." And she listened. She listened to how fraught with ineptitude and frustration a hospital stay can be. These were the very points she wanted to cover.

"And how long did it take to get your insurance payments settled?" To this, she got an earful. They were hooked.

The first five minutes of her twenty-minute talk were spent *listening.* She was able to base her comments on all that she had elicited. Her questions were not rhetorical. She worked with their answers. Her talk felt more like a dialogue than a monologue, even when she held the floor. And her business cards went flying off the table—more so than for any other speaker in the room.

■ ■ ■ ■ ■

Yet another way to start is with a personal anecdote, revealing your own humanity. Jane Goodall's memorable keynote speech mentioned earlier did just that. She began describing the origins of her curiosity about animals. While still a very small child, perhaps around two years old, she took a handful of earthworms to bed with her, wanting to study them at night. Her mother, upon discovering the earthworms in bed with her daughter, did not chastise or punish. She simply explained that the worms would die there—that they needed the earth to live in. So the two of them carried the worms in cupped hands back into the garden. Jane's theme was how important a force her mother was in her life and how she owed so much of what she accomplished to her mother's attitude. But instead of moralizing about this, she told several stories that left us wishing we all had had mothers like hers.

Jane Goodall is known for personalizing the study of chimpanzees. She gave them names. She described their personalities. It was all considered most unscientific at the time. But over time, she changed the face of scientific inquiry—by humanizing it.

■ ■ ■ ■ ■

Yet another option for beginning a talk is to quote a startling fact, one that will grab people's attention: "Ten years! Just ten years! That's all we have according to scientists studying global warming. In a mere ten years, we will have crossed the tipping point for disaster. If we don't start acting now, it will soon be too late!" However you begin, your own attitude will make or break the outcome of your talk.

Remember this: Your audience *wants* to like you. They want you to succeed. They sit back and breathe a sign of relief when it looks like you can command the room. They are on your side. Even the apathetic ones, the tired ones, would love to come alive if you can help them do so. No one sits there wishing you to fail. No one wants to be disappointed. So the more you do to show that you're on *their* side, the more you'll feel the connection and the more your own confidence will bloom.

Public speaking is truly a two-way street. You may think you're all alone up there, but your audience is truly with you, if you let them be. Real connection will make the podium a less lonely place—indeed, a place that can feel like home.

So let the Law of Attraction work for you. (It will anyway, so you may as well set the right intention.) Set your fears aside. Assume success. Whatever you focus on expands, so expand your repertory of successful results. See yourself as enjoying the spotlight; see yourself as connecting from your heart; picture a standing ovation. And then *practice, practice, practice!*

> *"As you climb your ladder of success,*
> *reach down and pull others along with you.*
> *You'll be in good company when you arrive."*
> —Saskia

PowerPoint vs. Personal Power

In the days of the dinosaurs, before PowerPoint, those who were asked to present usually had skills that made them worth listening to. After PowerPoint invaded our lives, the whole world was expected to make presentations. After all, anyone can put together a bunch of slides with bullet points. You don't even have to be a good writer!

The problem is most presenters don't have a clue as to how many slides can be covered in the time allotted. And they proceed to bore us to death by simply reading aloud what the audience is also reading—except that the audience is reading faster and is tuning out the presenter. Does this sound familiar?

This odd behavior may come from those who claim that they eye and the ear should reinforce the message. That some people learn aurally and some visually. Moreover, the insecure, reluctant presenter thinks she can hide behind slides and disappear. And indeed, this is true. But I ask: "If you are hiding, why should we be listening?"

The fact is: in public speaking, *when you set up a contest between the ear and the eye, the eye will always prevail.* No one will be listening while you are reading what we can also read, so why are you there at all?

When a client shows up with forty slides for a thirty-minute presentation, I know what my job is—to disabuse her of the notion that the slides constitute a story. Slides don't talk. People do. The speaker should have the audience's focus, not the slide show. But if you must use slides, here's the trick: Coordinate your voice and the slide so that they are *not* competing. Either show the image *first*—silently—and *then* comment on it.... Or... speak your piece and then show the slide to drive home the point.

PowerPoint is so prevalent that everyone feels they have to use it, whether they want to or not. Again, my advice is *tell a good story. Your personal power will far outshine a bunch of bullet points that compel your audience to tune you out.*

■ ■ ■ ■ ■

The Point of PowerPoint

I am not saying that PowerPoint is a useless tool. It can, in fact, be a great boon, assuming it is used as it was meant to be—as a *visual* aid. So make it visual! That means pictures, not paragraphs.

My favorite illustration comes from a long-standing client who was to host a conference on restructuring the electric utility industry in the United States. But she was off in another country advising that government on restructuring their own industry, leaving her no time to rehearse with me until the day before her keynote presentation. She asked me to look at her slides in advance of our only meeting. Normally, I don't want to see the slides before I watch how they are to be used, but in this case, having worked with her for years, I agreed.

When I received the slides, it was clear that her staff had sent the wrong package. Gone were the bar graphs, pie charts, and the numbers on which economists rely. Instead, I saw a Calder mobile, a pair of scissors, the Brooklyn Bridge, and a split-image of Katherine Hepburn—young and old.

At our rehearsal, I found to my delight, that the images I had received were not a mistake at all. How did she use them?

First, you must picture a sophisticated multimedia event with all possible technological bells and whistles. When she showed the Calder mobile, she compared it to the structure of the industry, carefully balanced, finely calibrated. Then the scissors moved in, snipping a small appendage, which quickly threw the mobile off balance.

She then presented her point: "If we fiddle with just a little piece of the industry without considering how it would affect the whole, we run the risk of throwing the entire thing out of whack." The visual aid conveyed her message twenty times more efficiently than words alone could have done. (Note, too, that the point was made using a potent analogy.)

She then showed a film of a bridge imploding, accompanied by thunderous sound effects, pointing out how disaster strikes when a structure is unsound. This was followed by a photo of the Brooklyn Bridge, a structure of elegance that has stood the test of time.

And last came the split-image of Katherine Hepburn, beautiful in her thirties and beautiful in her sixties. The closing remark: "As you can see, good bones last a lifetime!"

■ ■ ■ ■ ■

Bravo! Every part of this speech exemplified the perfect use of PowerPoint. Having heard this presentation only once, I can say in all honesty that the only reason I recall it after several years is that the imagery stayed with me, and thus, so did the message.

I hope you take away from this that *your slides should never replace you*. They should support, illustrate, entertain. But they are not there as a shield for you to hide behind.

As much as I would like to take credit for the "good bones" presentation, my client did it on her own. I may plant the seeds for how to tell a story, but my clients' creativity and imagination surprise me all the time. If clients resist, it is not because they don't trust me; it is that they don't yet trust themselves. They often think that because they have not yet unearthed their passion, it does not exist. But I've seen that when they finally do discover what excites them, they are unstoppable.

Can Numbers Tell Stories?

I have worked extensively with financial wizards. They love precision, and numbers are their language. But numbers don't tell stories—people do. Numbers just sit there looking important to some, unintelligible to others, and forgettable to most. And let's face it, after three decimal points, nobody cares. Numbers rely on interpretation, as illustrated below.

In the 1980s, after the near meltdown at Three-Mile Island nuclear plant, hearings were held to help determine damages. One of my clients was to testify early the first morning, so we traveled together late the night before and were mighty tired when the hearings began at 8:00 A.M. But no one was more tired-looking than the judge, who had probably spent many a late night dealing with this crisis.

As the day began, the judge was reclining flat out in his swivel chair. If he had been any more prone, he would have been invisible from below the raised platform. As it was, only his head could be seen from behind his massive desk. As the proceedings continued, I saw something that resembled a slow-motion film.

As my client became more impassioned about the right way to assess the damages, the judge started to come to life. His body shifted. He sat up just a bit straighter. Every few minutes, he kept inching forward, sitting up taller, until he was leaning forward on his elbows, nodding in agreement with what he was hearing. The movements were subtle, but the results dramatic.

My client was so busy with his story that he wasn't conscious of the judge's posture until I pointed it out to him afterwards. But he was subconsciously taking his cues from the look of interest on the judge's face. Connection begets connection! By the end of the hour, the judge looked like he had gotten a shot of adrenaline—from the expert's passion.

Given the judge's fatigue at the outset, if the expert had gone through a list of disembodied figures, it would have been a torturous morning. But he knew better. This man was a born storyteller—despite his Ph.D. in economics! He knew that *numbers make sense only if they tell a story.*

I once saw a researcher bring him a computer printout that must have been ten inches tall. My client flipped through the pages in a matter of minutes, his eyes traveling quickly down the columns. About halfway through, he pointed to a number and said to the researcher: "That can't be right!" They discussed it for a few seconds and the researcher left, looking a bit overwhelmed.

Later that morning, I overheard the same researcher in the elevator commenting on the incident to his buddies. Shaking his head in disbelief, he said: "I just don't know how he does it. I work for days, and he spots the one flaw in a matter of seconds!"

I wondered, too. So I asked my client how he could glance so quickly at so many figures and spot the one that didn't make sense. His words were memorable: "The numbers are not random, no matter how many pages they take up. They show a pattern…they tell a story. If the story is out of order, it doesn't add up. It can't make sense."

Part III: The Details

I gained insight that day into the similarities between his work and mine (and why we worked together so well): I was looking for the story in his facts; he was looking for the story in the numbers. When the two came together, the audience was always the winner.

Grown-ups like numbers.
When you tell them about a new
friend, they never ask questions
about what really matters.
They never ask:
"What does his voice sound like?"
"What games does he like best?"
"Does he collect butterflies?"
They ask:
"How old is he?"
"How many brothers does he have?"
"How much money does his father make?"
Only then do they think they know him.
—The Little Prince
Antoine de St. Exupery

IV.
IT'S A WRAP

*"Why settle for good
if you can be great?"*
—*It's the Thought That Counts*

A Note on the Keynote

All speakers are not created equal. That is a good thing!

Some are natural communicators; others do it despite their natural inclinations. Some are humorous, while others shy away from humor, feeling it's just not their style. Some see their job as instructing; others as entertaining. Still others are there to persuade you to buy, invest, or support their cause. The purposes and styles can be as varied as the speakers themselves.

Keynote speakers, however, are different. They may be just as varied as the others, but one trait distinguishes them: We want not only to *hear* what they say, we want to *understand* what makes them tick. We want to be moved, inspired, elevated by their words—and most of all by *who they are*. We want to understand their decisions, share their triumphs, spend a bit of time in their hearts and minds. And so, to be effective, they must open their hearts as well as their minds.

Keynote speakers must embody the values and experiences they describe. Their words are only as valid as their actions. An embattled corporate leader whose tactics are cut-throat cannot take the stage and speak about cooperation. A leader whose behavior belies his words will never have any clout. Not only will the media, the press, and the bloggers sniff out the truth, the speaker himself will give clues that reveal his lack of sincerity and credibility.

A keynote must inspire, share a vision, engage people, encourage creativity. A keynote must light our fire! *A keynote speaker is more than someone we want to hear: a keynote is someone we wish to be like.* To understand this, we must understand the difference between motivating and inspiring others: we are motivated by fear—by the negative consequences that follow a lack of action. ("If I don't get to the gym, I'll get flabby; if I don't watch my weight, I'll get fat.") But we are inspired by a positive force—by the good we derive from doing the right thing. ("I want to exercise because it makes me feel powerful and healthy; I watch my diet because I want to live the best life I can.")

The secret to a good keynote is the secret for all speakers: *Know thyself!* Know what you stand for; know what you would fight for. Only when you know yourself can you know what you want to say to inspire others. And only then will your authenticity speak volumes. This is where silence comes in to play.

In silence, you cultivate being, not doing. You gain insight into who you are. You work on internal clarity and cohesion, unlike the outer world, where you function awash in confusion and fragmentation.

I have been coaching leaders in industry, the law, economics, and the arts for more than twenty-eight years. I don't mean to imply that the minute I meet a client, we sit down and delve deeply into his soul. It is a gradual process—one in which trust grows on both sides. But in a remarkably short time, if the chemistry is right, we peel away the layers that hide what is true and sincere. And since I don't believe that the process is the same for all, I hope to convince you that a coach, while helpful, is not essential. You have everything within you to do the work on your own.

The work requires a commitment to looking within. Some choose meditation; some prefer yoga; some would rather seek renewal in nature; some, in taking a hot bath.

Whatever your path, make it a daily commitment, even if all you can spare is ten minutes.

What I've learned is that turning inward on a regular basis, and deepening your awareness set the stage for effective speaking. You can read books on speaking, take courses, attend seminars and workshops—all of which can help. But *until you face yourself, you will not have the confidence to face your audience.* And once you do face yourself, you will have so much more to share—your personal truth.

Hecklers and
Other Blessings

W ords can inspire or just take up time. We select keynote speakers not just for what they know but for what they have lived. Let me share a personal story, one that brought me clarity about why some speakers leave a mark and others fade away.

I was asked to be the keynote before a group working in the fine arts. The topic of the evening was "The Psychology of Creativity." After accepting the engagement, I hung up the phone and said to myself: "How am I, a speaking coach, going to make my message relevant to a group of painters?" Then I realized that going within, confronting themselves, was what artists did each time they faced a blank canvas. So I spent a few minutes before the group explicitly making the connection between how a speaker prepares and how a painter prepares.

The audience was right with me. I could feel it in the air. I could see it in their faces.

Feeling confident, I stopped to see if anyone had any questions. And indeed, one gentleman had a *hostile* question—certainly not what I had expected, nor apparently had the rest of the audience. He had come expecting the talk to be about art , and so he questioned the relevance of my topic. He was quickly perceived as a heckler, and the moderator tried to quiet him. I felt the audience throwing darts at him with their eyes and could see the whole talk spiraling out of control. I took action, without even planning what to do. First, I thanked the moderator for trying to give me back the floor, but I knew that I had to take it back on my own. Then I quieted the audience by saying that the man had a valid point and I wanted to address it. I shifted from his complaint to the purpose of my being there, and read from my book the opening passage, on silence. He calmed down and was not heard from for the rest of the evening.

But the most telling part of the incident came after the talk. Several people came up to me applauding how well I handled that touchy moment. In fact, some people were so impressed that they signed up for coaching, saying that they wanted to learn how to stay calm in the face of such events. Only a few commented on the content of my talk (which I thought was pretty good). Most continued marveling at how I diffused the comments of the heckler.

Ironically, I received a phone call two days later from the heckler himself, apologizing for his behavior, telling me he did not mean to be rude. I was most appreciative that he took the time to call, and it made me all the more convinced that if I had not respected his remarks, he never would have bothered making the effort to reach me.

So let me conclude with this.

If this book helps you think more clearly, I'll be happy.

If this book helps you act more sincerely, I'll be delighted.

And if this book helps you dig into your heart, mine the heart of your topic, and move the hearts of your audience, I'll know my job has been done.

"One sees clearly only with the heart.
Anything essential is invisible to the eyes."
—Antoine de St. Exupery

The Lesson in a Nightmare

This last story sums up all that I've been writing about. When the twin towers of the World Trade Center were attacked on September 11, Marsh & McLennan lost close to three hundred people. Its new CEO, Jeff Greenberg, on the job just a few months when this horror occurred, asked me to listen to the remarks he was preparing for the memorial service to be held in St. Patrick's Cathedral. It was to be broadcast to their fifty thousand employees around the world, and he wanted my thoughts on his brief comments.

I was deeply honored, and like all New Yorkers, deeply emotional. I was concerned that I wouldn't be able to contain my emotions during our rehearsal. I slept fitfully the night before, wondering how I would ever get through the session dry-eyed. I needn't have worried. Once I listened to Jeff's heartfelt words, I knew his entire audience would be crying, touched by his sincerity and his own emotion. As I sat there quietly weeping, I knew I was forecasting the reaction he would see in others the following day.

In previous talks, I had worked with him on word choice, pacing, delivery—the usual refinements of public speaking. In this case, I was speechless. When he was finished, I had only four words to say: "Don't change a word!"

He seemed surprised. "But what about my delivery?" he asked.

"Don't change a thing," was all I could find to tell him.

I had worked with three CEOs at Marsh over the previous fifteen years. Never had I left a session without finding something to polish, clarify, or improve. But I experienced something rare with Jeff Greenberg that day, and I know it was a lesson that bears remembering:

When you open your heart and talk from a place deep within you, the usual issues that bog down a speech simply vanish.

Jeff was broken open, as we all were, by the events of 9/11. Sometimes it takes living through a nightmare for us to reveal our kindest parts. Wouldn't it change us all if we could open up to what is real…to what counts…without the nightmare?

"Everybody lies most of the time,
but most of the time nobody is listening."
—After Dinner Speeches

Henry and Oprah

I heard a story in my early days as a coach that left a strong impression on me. I have no idea if it is true, but here it is:

A young intern working in the Nixon White House reported to Henry Kissinger. The intern's job was to research policy issues. One day he handed his first paper to Dr. Kissinger. An hour later, Dr. Kissinger handed it back to the intern, asking him: "Is this the best you can do?" The young man returned to his desk and worked on it until the end of the day.

The next morning, he left it for Dr. Kissinger, and again that same afternoon, got it back with a note: "Is this the best you can do?" Again, he polished it and turned it in a third time. Once again, Dr. Kissinger asked him: "Is this the best you can do?" This time he answered, "Yes, Dr. Kissinger, this is the very best I can do."

"Okay, now I'll read it!" said Henry Kissinger.

■ ■ ■ ■ ■

In a similar vein, I once watched a young woman, perhaps twenty years old, get up on Oprah and enthusiastically announce that her dream in life was to be the next Oprah. To this, Oprah responded: "Don't try to be me. Be the best *you*. I've got Oprah down pat. You can't do me as well as I can, so be whoever *you* are."

What classic advice. And so my plea to you is: Be your best self. On stage and off. For you really have no choice. You *can't* be anyone else. And if you try, *a poor imitation of someone else will never be as convincing as the real you*. Don't waste your time emulating even the best role models. Be who you are. Spend time in silence to find out who you are. Not who your job says you are; not who your spouse says you are; not who anyone living outside of your skin says you are.

Once you uncover the real you, you won't have to work at being fabulous...you won't be able to be anything less!

> *"Multitasking: Screwing up several*
> *things at once."*
> —*After Dinner Speeches*

Saskia's Secrets

When I started out, I felt compelled to make up my own rules for public speaking only to learn that there really aren't any rules. Like snowflakes, no two humans are alike. Therefore, the so-called rules have to bend around who you are, how you think, what you value, and how you differ from everyone else.

Don't let anyone (including me) tell you, "This is the way it is done!" There is no way. There are only ways. And the more you feel at home in the way you've chosen, the more you know it is the right fit.

My secrets are few:

1. Silence
2. Story
3. Simplicity
4. Sincerity

Of course, none of them is a secret at all. (But…shhh…don't tell anyone!)

I'd like to leave you with these final thoughts on silence, spirit, and speaking.

Sit in Silence

Call it meditation. Call it contemplation. Call it calming the mind. Call it what you will. But spend time in silence every day. You will meet your intuition there. It is often said that prayer is where you talk to God; meditation is where God talks to you (if only you'll listen).

Listen in Silence

When you listen, learn to be fully present; don't react; don't plan your response; don't judge; don't evaluate. Just be.

Trust in Silence

In your talks, be they formal or informal—
Pause. Breathe.
Let what you say sink in.
Don't rush ahead.

Give the ear the equivalent of white space on a page...silence...shhh!
And finally, always remember: *Less is more.*

And in Conclusion...

*A*nd *in conclusion.* These are probably the favorite words of anyone listening to a speech.

Let *me* conclude by wishing you this in your life as a public speaker:

- Enjoy yourself! Have fun! Nothing will ensure success more.
- Find your voice and stick to it.
- Forget about performing. Think about being.
- Forget about pleasing others. Please yourself.
- Know what makes you come alive and tap into that source.
- Forget about fear. It can't stand up to fun.
- Know that the public you is a reflection of the private you. Take your assets and flaunt them.
- Know that you can choose to be fearless. You can choose to be sincere. You can choose joy.

Then:
- You will be chosen—to speak, to lead, to inspire.

My last wish for you is that the *least* favorite words of *your* audiences will be: "And in conclusion..."

Bibliography

Included here are some academic or technical books related to my field of linguistics. But if you are seeking further support in finding your voice, I would steer you to the more popular or spiritual books that take you on a journey to the heart.

Albom, Mitch. *Tuesdays with Morrie: An Old Man, a Young Man, and Life's Greatest Lesson.* New York: Time Warner Paperbacks, 2003.

Berg, Elizabeth. *Escaping Into the Open: The Art of Writing True.* New York: HarperCollins, 2000.

Boorstein, Sylvia, Ph.D. *Happiness is an Inside Job: Practicing for a Joyful Life.* New York: Ballantine Books, 2007.

Boorstein, Sylvia, Ph.D. *It's Easier Than You Think: The Buddhist Way to Happiness.* New York: HarperCollins, 1995.

Braden, Gregg. *The Divine Matrix: Bridging Time, Space, Miracles, and Belief.* Carlsbad, CA: Hay House, Incorporated, 2008.

Bryson, Bill. *The Penguin Dictionary of Troublesome Words.* New York: Penguin Group, 1984.

Chomsky, Noam. *Language and Mind.* New York: Cambridge University Press, 2006.

Collins, Jim. *Good to Great: Why Some Companies Make the Leap...and Others Don't.* New York: HarperCollins, 2001.

Dalai Lama. *An Open Heart: Practicing Compassion in Everyday Life.* New York: Little Brown & Company, 2001.

De Angelis, Barbara. *Real Moments: Discover the Secret for True Happiness.* New York: Dell Publishing, 1995.

Detz, Joan. *How to Write and Give a Speech: A Practical Guide.* New York: St. Martin's Press, 1984.

Di Vesta, Francis J. *Language, Learning, and Cognitive Processes (Basic Concepts in Educational Psychology Series).* Belmont, CA: Wadsworth Publishing Company, 1974.

Elbow, Peter. *Writing Without Teachers.* New York: Oxford University Press, 1973.

Gilbert, Daniel. *Stumbling on Happiness.* New York: Vintage Books, 2007.

Gilbert, Elizabeth. *Eat, Pray, Love: One Woman's Search for Everything Across Italy, India and Indonesia.* New York: Penguin, 2007.

Gladwell, Malcolm. *The Tipping Point: How Little Things Can Make a Big Difference.* New York: Little Brown & Company, 2000.

———. *Blink: The Power of Thinking Without Thinking.* New York: Little Brown & Company, 2007.

Gunning, Robert. *The Technique of Clear Writing.* New York: McGraw-Hill, 1968.

Hembrough, Alan D. and Frank K. Sonnenberg. *It's the Thought That Counts: Over 500 Thought-Provoking Lessons to Inspire a Richer Life.* Provo, UT: Executive Excellence Publishing, 2001.

Hicks, Esther, and Jerry Hicks. *Ask and It Is Given: Learning to Manifest Your Desires.* Carlsbad, CA: Hay House, 2005.

Hurd, Hollis T. *Writing for Lawyers.* Pittsburgh: Journal Broadcasting & Communications, 1982.

La Mott, Anne. *Bird by Bird: Some Instructions on Writing and Life.* New York: Knopf Publishing Group, 1995.

Bibliography

Lesser, Elizabeth. *The Seeker's Guide: Making Your Life a Spiritual Adventure.* New York: Villard Books, 2000.

———. *Broken Open: How Difficult Times Can Help Us Grow.* New York: Villard Books, 2005.

Levoy, Gregg Michael. *Callings: Finding and Following an Authentic Life.* New York: Three Rivers Press, 1998.

Maisel, Eric. *A Writer's Paris: A Guided Journey for the Creative Soul.* Cincinnati: Writer's Digest Books, 2005.

Mitchell, Richard. *Less Than Words Can Say: The Underground Grammarian.* New York: Little Brown & Company, 1979.

Mitchell, Stephen. *Tao Te Ching.* New York: Harper Perennial, 1992.

Noonan, Peggy. *On Speaking Well: How to Give a Speech with Style, Substance, and Clarity.* New York: ReganBooks, 1999.

Petras, Kathryn, and Ross Petras. *Age Doesn't Matter Unless You're a Cheese: Wisdom from Our Elders.* New York: Workman Publishing Company, 2002.

Pink, Daniel H. *A Whole New Mind: Moving from the Information Age to the Conceptual Age.* New York: Riverhead Books, 2005.

Postman, Neil. *Crazy Talk, Stupid Talk: How We Defeat Ourselves by the Way We Talk and What to Do About It.* New York: Delacorte Press, 1976.

———. *Amusing Ourselves to Death: Public Discourse in the Age of Show Business.* New York: Penguin Books, 1985.

Remen, Rachel Naomi. *Kitchen Table Wisdom: Stories That Heal.* New York: Riverhead Books, 1996.

———. *My Grandfather's Blessings: Stories of Strength, Refuge, and Belonging.* New York: Riverhead Books, 2001.

Rico, Gabriele Lusser. *Writing the Natural Way: Turn the Task of Writing into the Joy of Writing.* New York: J.P. Tarcher, 1983.

Stokes, Jamie, ed. *The Little Book of After Dinner Speeches*. New York: Barnes & Noble Books. 2002.

Strunk, William, Jr., and E. B. White. *The Elements of Style*. New York: Macmillan Paperbacks, 1962.

Tannen, Deborah. *You Just Don't Understand: Women and Men in Conversation*. New York: Ballantine Books, 1990.

Tarshis, Barry. *How to Write Like a Pro*. New York: Plume, 1983.

Tolle, Eckhart. *A New Earth: Awakening to Your Life's Purpose*. New York: Dutton Adult, 2005.

Ueland, Brenda. *If You Want to Write: A Book about Art, Independence and Spirit*. Saint Paul, MN: Graywolf Press, 1938.

Vanzant, Iyanla. *In the Meantime: Finding Yourself and the Love You Want*. New York: Simon & Schuster Adult Publishing Group, 1998.

Waitzkin, Josh. *The Art of Learning: A Journey in the Pursuit of Excellence*. New York: Free Press, 2007.

Walsh, Neale Donald. *Conversations with God, Bk. 1: An Uncommon Dialogue*. Charlottesville, VA: Hampton Roads Publishing Company, 1997.

Williamson, Marianne. *Enchanted Love: The Mystical Power of Intimate Relationships*. New York: Touchstone, 1999.

Wydick, Richard C. *Plain English for Lawyers*, 2nd ed. Durham, NC: Carolina Academic Press, 1985.

Zander, Benjamin, and Rosamund Stone Zander. *The Art of Possibility: Transforming Professional and Personal Life*. New York: Penguin Books, 2000.

Zinsser, William. *On Writing Well: The Classic Guide to Writing Nonfiction*. New York: HarperResource, 2006.

———. *Writing to Learn*. New York: Harper & Row, 1988.

Index

Abraham-Hicks, 19–20, 103
actions versus outcome, 7
After Dinner Speeches, 29, 57,
    65, 75, 151, 153
analogy, 135
    the perfect, 95–97
    the power of, 96–97
analysis, 72
anecdote, personal, opening
    speech with, 129, 130–131
anxiety, performance, 59–61
"Are You Listening to Your
    Echo?", 53–54
attitude, 33, 59, 131
audience, 5, 6, 29, 32, 33, 37,
    41, 42, 51, 56, 63, 64, 65,
    66, 69, 71, 72, 73, 75, 76,
    77, 80, 83, 85, 86, 92, 93,
    95, 100, 101, 103, 104,
    108, 109, 112, 113, 120,
    124, 125, 126, 127, 128,
    129, 130, 131, 132, 133,
    134, 139, 145, 147, 148,
    149, 155
    ensuring a captive, 106–
    107

    knowing the, 106
authenticity, 94, 115, 119, 144

body language, 32, 33, 51, 75–
    77, 103, 120
    reading, 51
brain cells, and connection to
    gut, 52
brain, shutting down of the,
    105–106
Brandeis, Louis D., 111
bravado, 39–40
Brooklyn Bridge, the, 134

Calder mobile, 134, 135
Cassandra, 130
Catered Affair, A, 117
causation and correlation,
    distinction between, 95–96
charisma, 34
chemistry, 41, 144
Chopra, Deepak, 54, 86
cleverness, versus wisdom, 37–38
Columbia University, 39
communication, the key to,
    83–84

communicator, what makes a good, 51–52

confidence, 4, 8, 9, 12, 26, 29–30, 32, 35, 63, 65, 66, 75, 101, 108, 131, 145

Course in Miracles, A, 54

Crazy Talk, Stupid Talk, 100

credibility, 32–33, 34, 42, 144

Dam, Ras, 123

data collection, 72

de St. Exupery, Antoine, 13, 17, 93, 101, 119, 139, 149

delivery, 71, 149, 150

dialogue, private, versus public monologue, 55–56

Educational Solutions, 13

Einstein, Albert, 37, 85, 95

embarrassment, 63 (*see also* fear)

emotional intelligence (EQ), 109–110

energy, vibrational, 20

English as a Second Language, 14

Enron, 42

enthusiasm, 31, 32

Ephron, Nora, 126

expertise, 32–33

eye contact, 103–104

fear, 5, 8, 9, 12, 19, 20, 27, 34, 57–58, 58–61, 63–64, 80, 89, 92, 99, 104, 107, 113, 116, 118, 120, 132, 144, 155

of speaking, and spiritual aspect of, 4, 9

tackling, 60–61

fun, 29–30, 85–86

Gathering, The, 117

Gattegno, Dr. Caleb, 13, 39, 45–47

goals, 121, 123–124, 129

Goodall, Jane, Ph.D., 101, 130–131

Greenberg, Jeff, 149–150

Hamlet, 104

Hepburn, Katherine, 134, 135

Hope, Bob, 128

humanity, 37

showing one's, 109–110

humor, 66, 68, 87, 100, 125, 129

opening speech with, 128–129

"I Have a Dream" speech, 93

It's the Thought That Counts, 7, 11, 23, 31, 39, 63, 79, 85, 89, 115, 123, 137, 143

integrity, 26, 34–35,

jargon, 112

Johnson, Samuel, 125

joke, opening, 128

joy, 59

King, Martin Luther, Jr., 93

Kissinger, Dr. Henry, 151–152

knowledge, three stages of, 72

Kripalu, 105

language, 13–16
  processing of, 105
Law of Attraction, the, 19–21,
  43, 81, 83, 89, 118, 132
listeners, engaging, 83, 84, 86,
  105–106, 110, 120, 125–
  132
listening, 4, 7, 16, 26, 45–47,
  51, 53, 68, 93, 100, 109,
  119, 130, 133, 151, 155
Little Prince, The, 139

Magic Hands Freddy, 117
Marsh & McLennan, 149
meditation, 12, 20, 89, 144,
  154
memory:
  long-term, 105
  short-term, 105
Michelangelo, 6
monologue, public, versus
  private dialogue, 55–56

9/11, 149–150
New York University, 100
News Hour, 76
Ninn, Anais, 19
notes, being tied to, 111

Olivier, Laurence, 99
Omega Institute, the, 101, 126
Oprah (see Winfrey, Oprah)

passion, 20, 29, 32, 34, 40, 43,
  56, 63, 73, 79, 100, 107,

108, 120, 136, 138
  discovering one's own, 8, 9
patience, 15
PBS, 76
Pemberthy, John, 99
philosophy:
  maturation of, 34
  three-legged, 31–35
Piaget, Dr. Jean, 13
Plain English, Please!, 41
pornography, definition of by
  Supreme Court, 75
Postman, Neil, 100
PowerPoint, 66, 133–136
preparation, 4, 6, 12, 20, 21,
  69, 75, 108
  lack of, 66
presence, 30, 34, 60, 69, 101,
  109
Proctor, Bob, 118
public speaking, definition of,
  57–58, 71–73

reading aloud, problems with,
  100
Rolls Royce, 96

Sai Baba, Shirdi, 105
Seinfeld, Jerry, 5
self-worth, sense of, 25
Shakespeare, William, 104
Shaw, Arje, 117–118
Shaw, Esther, 117, 118
shortcuts, lack of, 65
silence, 11–12, 13–16, 17, 18,
  20, 21, 25, 46, 47, 63, 69,
  81, 89, 104, 128, 144, 148,

152, 153, 154
Silent Way, the, 13–16, 39, 45
simplicity, 153
slides, and use of during
    speaking, 133–136 (*see also*
    PowerPoint)
speaker, keynote, 143–145
speaking, being yourself while,
    7
speech openers, 125–132
spirit, wakefulness of, 105–106
spontaneity, 32, 65–66, 67–69
St. Patrick's Cathedral, 149
statistics, opening speech with,
    131–132
story, 8, 29, 31, 33, 42, 61, 63,
    71, 80, 89–92, 93–94, 95–
    97, 99, 101, 104, 106, 126,
    129, 134, 136, 138–139,
    153
    importance of, 17–18
    telling versus reading, 99–
    100
    the making of a good, 91–
    92
Streep, Meryl, 99–100
success, 7
synthesis, 72

technocrat, 105
Temple, Shirley, 129
theme, 93–94
thinking, negative, awareness
    of, 8
thought, versus silence, 12
Three-Mile Island, 137
To Bee or Not to Bee, 99

traits, common shared by
    public speakers, 31–35
truth, 18, 30, 33, 42, 43, 46,
    51, 89, 103, 105, 107, 113,
    119, 120, 143, 145
    power of, 113
Twain, Mark, 9

vision, 5, 9, 107, 109, 114
    finding one's own, 23–27
visual aids (see slides)
voice, 5, 34, 42, 55, 69, 100,
    104, 113, 119, 134
    finding one's own, 6, 7–8,
    16, 23–27, 43, 51, 52,
    119–121, 155, 157

Winfrey, Oprah, 151–152
wisdom, versus cleverness, 37–
    38
World Trade Center, the, 149
writer's block, 79–81

yoga, 21, 105, 119–121, 144